The Train:
A Model for Transforming the Heart

Vincent L. Wood

DEDICATION

I dedicate this work to Robin, my dear wife. I love you and thank God for your influence on my life and on the lives of our family. You have faithfully shown me Jesus' love for over thirty years. You model a life of faith for our family, and the churches we have served. I am deeply thankful for the way that you love and honor my mother. You are a tremendous woman. Thank you for continually encouraging me to press on.

CONTENTS

Acknowledgments   i

Introduction   iii

1   Anger   3

2   My Needs   21

3   The Heart   39

4   The Train   51

5   Fear and Guilt   63

6   Philippians 4:6-9   75

7   Shields   85

8   Now What?   95

9   Obstacles   109

10   Self-Protective Strategies   119

11   Hope   127

12   Process   139

Appendix: Discipleship Plan   149

Bibliography   159

ACKNOWLEDGMENTS

The single greatest support and encouragement in my life and ministry has been Robin Wood. Robin saw and spoke the value in my thoughts and provided me with the hope and time to devote to research and articulation of my thoughts. In addition, Randy Steele got me started on this path by mentoring me and trusting me enough to allow me to develop my shepherding skills. Erin Evans gave the initial editing and formatting help. Britney Wood provided invaluable assistance in editing. Finally, Kate Horst of Purple Parachute provided some of the artwork. Patrick and Michael, my sons, are the pride of my life. They endured countless discussion of these ideas, have sought to implement them in their own lives, and have allowed me to share some of their thoughts. Thank you all for your love and support.

VINCENT L. WOOD

INTRODUCTION

Watch over your heart with all diligence, for from it flow the springs of life.
Proverbs 4:23

"Everyone is insecure. We just express it in different ways." A missionary made this statement to a group of newly approved missionaries preparing to begin fund-raising. She was discussing some of the problems in her family when she made this astute observation. The simplicity and profundity of the statement is striking. As the people of God grasp the ramifications of this simple statement, they will be better prepared to impact themselves, and those around them, in meaningful ways.

What is insecurity? Insecurity is a lack of confidence in one's personal safety or value. It has to do with one's beliefs more than it has to do with reality. Dustin Hoffman is regarded as one of the finest actors in Hollywood today.[1] His ability to accurately portray characters as diverse as an autistic adult, a cross-dressing actor, a renowned professor of literature, and even Captain Hook is astounding. Following an interview with Mr. Hoffman, Nigel Farnsdale wrote that Hoffman is "a perfectionist who fears being exposed as a fraud if he turns in what he believes is a second-rate performance..."[2] Dustin Hoffman illustrates that sometimes

---

[1] Chris Walczyk 2012, "Top 100 Greatest Actors of All Time (The Ultimate List)" Internet Movie Database. accessed December 17, 2014. http://www.imdb.com/list/ls050274118/

[2] Nigel Farnsdale, 2003. "The Trials of Hoffman" The Telegraph, accessed December 17, 2014. http://www.telegraph.co.uk/culture/film/3590080/The-trials-of-Hoffman.html

insecurity has nothing to do with reality but instead with one's personal perceptions and beliefs.

Truth is an objective reality that demands our conformity. However, in the postmodern mindset, truth is divided into two categories: universal truths and personal truths. This division of truth is an expansion of Immanuel Kant's idea of phenomena and forms. Phenomena are that which we experience empirically. We understand these phenomena to the extent that our experience of them corresponds to the form, or universal reality. Two people sit on two different objects, and both call them chairs even though they are very different from one another. What constitutes a chair? Your idea of what qualifies as a chair may be quite different from another person's idea, and yet both are similar to the actual form of chair. Therefore, both people are correct, possessing different "truths" of what is a chair. This complex idea is simplified by stating, "We each have our own truth." Postmodern thought invites each person to live consistent with one's own perception of reality.

Such a lifestyle is doomed to fail because truth exists. Jesus said, "I am the way, the truth and the life…" Truth, simply stated, is God's perspective. What does the omniscient One think about a given situation? That is truth. He sees all sides and interprets the events accurately. He alone knows the thoughts and intentions of each individual involved. Success in life requires people to discover and conform to His perspective in every situation. To the extent that people do this, they will succeed. Conforming to God's perspective will also set people free from insecurity. Jesus said in John 8:32, "…you shall know the truth and the truth will set you free."

The drive for security is one of the most significant motivating factors in our lives. Every person desperately wants to be safe. Everyone needs to be safe. People hurt those they love, ignore those who love them, fight for position, lie, and even commit immoral acts all in an effort to feel safe. Even with all of these efforts, the fact remains that it is not working. It is not working because, for those of us who are Christians, we are already safe. We just do not consistently believe it. God loves His people and has sworn by Himself that He will never abandon them. The Creator of the heavens and the earth, the giver and sustainer of life, the almighty King of kings has sworn that nothing will ever separate His people from His love. How could anyone ever be safer?

Yet we continually strive to find other people who will love us. God commands man to love Him and love others. To enable our obedience to this command, He bestows His great love on us, thereby setting us free to love Him and those around us. Instead of expressing to others a measure of the love we have received, we often live as though our purpose is to be loved by people. Imagine a man in a war zone who lives in a concrete and steel bunker thirty feet underground. Each day he lives in terror of his enemies who only possess small handguns. His fear rises as he thinks about how safe he would feel if only he lived in a paper box out in the middle of the street. He thinks, "Oh, a paper box would be so secure. If only I had a paper box on the street, then I would be safe from the enemy's guns." This image is absurd, and yet it accurately illustrates the absurdity of the continual effort of sinful man to find security in the love of other sinful people.

The Train is an illustration of the heart, including the mind, the will, and the emotions. It is common to emphasize one aspect of the heart over another, considering the parts in isolation from one another. In this book, we will maintain a consistent understanding of the heart as the mind, will, and emotions. We will develop the truth that man's emotions *never* work apart from the mind and will, and that they are *always* a response to what a person is thinking and believing. This tenacious commitment to these simple propositions will enable us to trust our emotions. We will not trust our emotions to be sensors that warn of danger. Instead, our emotions indicate how well we remember and believe the profound truth the Jesus is all that we need.

The Train is a model based on biblical anthropology and is consistent with approved psychological understandings of how people succeed in life. I developed these concepts by studying the scriptures, theological works, and practical counseling techniques. This model has been tested by over two decades of pastoral counseling. In order to help understand the application of this model, most chapters will begin and end with a story (in italics). Some of these stories are real experiences of people who have used *The Train* model to grow in their faith. Some stories are a compilation of different people's experiences. In both cases, the names and other details have been changed to protect the identity of people whom I have counseled.

Section 1: Basic Principles

VINCENT L. WOOD

1 ANGER

Do not be eager in your heart to be angry,
for anger resides in the bosom of fools.
Ecclesiastes 7:9

"Honey, I'm home," Alan said with a chuckle as he remembered the old "I Love Lucy" show.

"Did you bring the milk?" Sally did not see the humor. She expected him to forget the milk and her words conveyed her disgust. She was sure that he wasn't really listening to her when she called and asked him to stop by the store on the way home.

"No, I'm sorry. I forgot."

"How am I supposed to finish dinner without the milk? We are out of paper towels too."

Alan sighed. *"I'll be right back."* He slammed the door and started the engine. He was pleased that the tires squealed as he pulled out of the driveway. *"I hope she heard that."*

When he came in the second time, Alan was not as jovial. He was mad. Sally had been demanding and rude. She should have at least greeted him before telling him to go to the store. Other men were greeted with a kiss when they came home. After all, He was working to provide for her so she could stay at home with the kids. During his twenty minute shopping trip, Alan kept replaying how Sally continually treated him like this. His anger *was just growing. It was not a pleasant dinner. Alan was short with Sally and the kids. He just wanted to get away before he blew up.*

Years ago, I asked my two sons, "Why do you get mad?" Without hesitation, they replied, "Because I don't get what I want." Theirs was a simple, honest, and deeply profound assessment of their hearts. At first glance, you may disagree. Each of us wants to believe that our anger is justified. The Christian, in particular, wants to assert that her anger is aimed at sin and therefore is righteous. Surely, with all of the years of disciplining ourself toward godliness, my anger stems from something more substantial than "not getting what I want." Or does it?

Is my anger wrong?

A careful examination of the Bible on the topic of anger reveals that righteous anger is much rarer than we would like to believe. It is essential, in order to properly understand God's perspective on anger, that we allow Scripture to guide our thoughts and not insert our opinions into the sacred text. A good place to start is with a short statement from Jesus' brother, James. James 1:20 reads, "for the anger of man does not achieve the righteousness of God." The Greek word translated as "righteousness" is δικαιοςύνη. Δικαιοςύνη means a life that conforms to a standard. According to the *Theological Dictionary of the New Testament,* the word δικαιοςύνη in the book of James is a "life in agreement with God's will."

James indicates, in no uncertain terms that man's anger does not advance God's desire. In fact, the anger of man does not conform to the will of God at all. If it does not accomplish God's righteousness, how can it ever be justified? Matthew Henry says about this verse, "Wrath is a human thing, and the wrath of man stands opposed to the righteousness of God."[3]

James uses the Greek word οργή which is most frequently

---

[3] Matthew Henry, Matthew Henry's Commentary Acts to Revelation (McLean MacDonald Publishing Company, 1985) 973

translated as wrath. *Opyή* is used thirty-six times in the *Nestle-Aland Greek New Testament 27th Edition.* Thirty of those are translated "wrath," and six times it is "anger" in the New American Standard Bible. Most frequently, *opyή* refers to the wrath of God. As such, *opyή* is an anger which is retributive in nature. God's wrath is an expression of His judgment extended as a punishment for violating His law (consider Romans 1:18[4]). The anger of man can be understood as an expression of wrath to "punish" another person for some offending action. James is pointing out that when people strike out to make someone pay for what they did, they fail to accomplish God's righteousness: they fail to conform to the desires of God. In part, this is true because God has reserved vengeance for Himself, the only righteous judge (Romans 12:19,[5] 1 Peter 2:23[6]).

Why do people express anger? Does not a man show anger in order to communicate his displeasure with someone or something? Does he not want that communication to motivate the recipient of his anger to cease and desist from their actions? This is the *opyή* of James 1:19-20. Man is sinful. "For all have sinned and fall short of the glory of God."[7] A judge who does not meet basic ethical standards can never be trusted to mete out true justice. When we, sinful men and women, usurp the role of judge, we prevent true righteousness from occurring.

James refers to the anger of man. Is it possible that some anger rises from the work of God in a man's heart and is therefore justified? In fact, to most people, their anger usually feels like it is righteous. Consider Galatians 5:16-23:

> But I say, walk by the Spirit, and you will not carry out the desire of the flesh. For the flesh sets its desire against the Spirit, and the Spirit against the flesh; for these are in opposition to one another, so

---

[4] Romans 1:18 "For the wrath of God is revealed from heaven against all ungodliness and unrighteousness of men who suppress the truth in unrighteousness," NASU

[5] Romans 12:19 "Never take your own revenge, beloved, but leave room for the wrath of God, for it is written, "VENGEANCE IS MINE, I WILL REPAY," says the Lord."

[6] 1 Peter 2:23 "and while being reviled, He did not revile in return; while suffering, He uttered no threats, but kept entrusting Himself to Him who judges righteously; "

[7] Romans 3:23

that you may not do the things that you please. But if you are led by the Spirit, you are not under the Law. Now the deeds of the flesh are evident, which are: immorality, impurity, sensuality, idolatry, sorcery, enmities, strife, jealousy, outbursts of anger, disputes, dissensions, factions, envying, drunkenness, carousing, and things like these, of which I forewarn you just as I have forewarned you that those who practice such things shall not inherit the kingdom of God. But the fruit of the Spirit is love, joy, peace, patience, kindness, goodness, faithfulness, gentleness, self-control; against such things there is no law.

In this passage, Paul contrasts the deeds of the flesh and the fruit of the Spirit. He points out the mutually exclusive character of each force in a person's life when he writes, "the flesh sets its desires against the Spirit." In the deeds of the flesh, Paul lists outbursts of anger. Anger is not ordinarily a work of God's Spirit. Instead, anger is most often an expression of a person's desire set against that of God's Spirit.

Consider these two similar passages. Ephesians 4:31 says, "Let all bitterness and wrath and anger and clamor and slander be put away from you, along with all malice." The Apostle Paul reiterates this idea in Colossians 3:8, "But now you also, put them all aside: anger, wrath, malice, slander, and abusive speech from your mouth." In these two passages, Paul instructs his readers to put aside all anger and wrath. It is of great importance to note that Paul, under the inspiration of the Spirit of God, tells the people of God to set aside all wrath and anger. He could have left out the word "all" and simply said "put aside anger and wrath." Had he chosen to do so, one might properly conclude that anger in general is bad but on occasion it is acceptable. When the Spirit led Paul to write "all" anger and wrath, He removed that option. God commands the removal of all anger and wrath.

John Calvin wrote in his commentary on Colossians 3:8 that the word translated as "wrath" is "θυμός—a term that denotes a more impetuous passionateness than *οργή*."[8] Vines Expository Dictionary comments on these two words.

> *θυμός* indicates a more agitated condition of the feelings, an outburst of wrath from inward indignation, while *οργή* suggests a more settled or abiding condition of mind, frequently with a view to taking revenge. *οργή* is less sudden in its rise than *θυμός*, but more lasting in its nature. *θυμός* expresses more the inward feeling, *οργή* the more active emotion.[9]

So Paul points out that whether the emotion of anger is a sudden explosion, or a settled resentment, it is to be removed from one's life.

In Ephesians 4:20-24 we read,

> [20] But you did not learn Christ in this way, [21] if indeed you have heard Him and have been taught in Him, just as truth is in Jesus, [22] that, in reference to your former manner of life, you lay aside the old self, which is being corrupted in accordance with the lusts of deceit, [23] and that you be renewed in the spirit of your mind, [24] and put on the new self, which in the likeness of God has been created in righteousness and holiness of the truth.

Paul reminds the Ephesians of the most basic of Christian principles: they are to lay aside the old self and put on the new self. Paul tells them to continually practice this life-changing pattern of repentance. The verses that follow are examples of how this pattern is lived out in the Christian's life.

In verse 25 Paul writes, "Therefore, laying aside falsehood, speak truth each one of you with his neighbor, for we are members of one another." The readers are to lay aside falsehood, which is

---

[8] John Calvin, Calvin's Commentary Vol XXI (Grand Rapids, 1981) 210
[9] Vine's Expository Dictionary of Biblical Words, (Nashville,Thomas Nelson Publishers, 1985) Biblesoft Inc.

clearly a part of the old self, and instead, putting on the new self, speak truth. The pattern of life changing repentance is seen in their truthful speech.

Ephesians 4:26 says, "Be angry and yet do not sin..." It seems, at first glance, that Paul is commanding the Ephesians to be angry at times. A.T. Robertson rightly notes that this is a "permissive imperative, not a command to be angry."[10] This is why the translators of the NIV chose to translate this verse, "In your anger do not sin." This interpretation makes the most sense when the context is taken into account. If the verse is indeed commanding people to be angry, it seems to violate Paul's words five verses later when he commands, "Let all bitterness and wrath and anger and clamor and slander be put away from you, along with all malice." Why would Paul command the Ephesians to be angry, only to tell them to remove it? That does not seem consistent with the flow of the passage.

So what does Paul mean? Look at the context again. Paul says, "Be angry and yet do not sin. Do not let the sun go down on your anger." Regardless of one's interpretation about the rightness of anger, it must be conceded that the end of verse 26 commands the readers to remove the anger from their lives before the end of the day. In the very verse that may contain a possible command to anger, one finds God telling the reader to set it aside quickly. Verse 27 explains why people need to get rid of anger quickly: "and do not give the devil an opportunity." Holding on-to the anger allows the devil to move in the heart and reap destruction. Why would God command anger, when anger provides the devil an opportunity in the Christian's life? Such a command would be like God commanding Adam and Eve to spend the day meditating on the Tree of the Knowledge of Good and Evil. As if He asked them to smell the fruit, touch it, bite into it, enjoying the texture and flavor without actually eating it. Would the God who is asked "lead us not into temptation" actually command his people to flirt with sin? Such a proposition is untenable. James 1:13 says, "Let

---

[10]A. T. Robertson, Robertson's Word Pictures in the New Testament, Electronic Database. Copyright © 1997, 2003, 2005, 2006 by Biblesoft, Inc. Robertson's Word Pictures in the New Testament. Copyright © 1985 by Broadman Press.)

no one say when he is tempted, 'I am being tempted by God'; for God cannot be tempted by evil, and He Himself does not tempt anyone."

As Paul continues his thoughts in Ephesians 4, he provides the solution to the dilemma.

> [28] He who steals must steal no longer; but rather he must labor, performing with his own hands what is good, so that he will have something to share with one who has need. [29] Let no unwholesome word proceed from your mouth, but only such a word as is good for edification according to the need of the moment, so that it will give grace to those who hear. [30] Do not grieve the Holy Spirit of God, by whom you were sealed for the day of redemption. [31] Let all bitterness and wrath and anger and clamor and slander be put away from you, along with all malice. [32] Be kind to one another, tender-hearted, forgiving each other, just as God in Christ also has forgiven you.

In verse 28 Paul addresses "him who steals," and tells him to stop and find something useful to do. In verse 29 he tells the readers to not speak unwholesomely, but with grace. In these two verses Paul gives a pattern. He instructs his readers to set aside a particular sin by choosing a good deed instead. It seems evident that Paul started this pattern in verse 26. He addresses three sins: anger, stealing and harmful words. In each, he mentions the presence of the sin in one's life and gives clear instruction to remove it. To strengthen this instruction, he continues in verse 30 with the exhortation to not grieve the Spirit of God. In verses 31-32, Paul expands the idea by telling the Ephesians to put aside a whole list of objectionable actions and replace them with the good deeds of kindness, tenderheartedness and forgiveness. By looking at the whole section, it seems most reasonable that Paul does not encourage, let alone command, anger. On the contrary, he gives a strategy to remove its destructive power from one's life.

Jesus gives valuable instruction regarding anger in Matthew 5:21-22,

> You have heard that the ancients were told, 'You shall not commit murder' and 'Whoever commits murder shall be liable to the court.' "But I say to you that everyone who is angry with his brother shall be guilty before the court; and whoever shall say to his brother, 'Raca,' shall be guilty before the supreme court; and whoever shall say, 'You fool,' shall be guilty enough to go into the fiery hell.

In this passage, Jesus points out that according to the accepted law of the day, murder leaves a person "liable to the court." He reminds His hearers of the culpability of one who murders another. That culpability is presented as being "liable to the court." Jesus then states that one who is angry is guilty before the court. In the Greek text, the wording is identical as Jesus describes the culpability. Both the murderer and the one who is angry are liable to the court. His point is that anger is a form of murder. He offers no qualifying circumstances which could make some murder justifiable. Remember the sentence instituted by God for murder in Genesis 9:6, "Whoever sheds man's blood, by man his blood shall be shed, for in the image of God He made man." Murder, from the time of Noah, was punishable by death because in the act of murder, a man strikes out against the image of God. Jesus gives the pattern followed throughout the New Testament, that our anger is not a godly trait but is instead an expression of the flesh and sinful.

What about the Old Testament? Is anger treated as sinful in the Old Testament? The Hebrew word for anger is חָרָר the *Theological Wordbook of the Old Testament* says that חָרָר means "to cause fire to burn." In the King James translation of Genesis 39:19, we read of Potipher that "his wrath was kindled." There is within anger a kindling inside of an individual. Most people have experienced this burning. One witnesses an offense, he meditates on the offensive nature of the action, he rehearses the event to remember the offense, until finally it becomes a fire inside his heart. Thus the Hebrews speak of anger as חָרָר "a burning."

Consider the books of Psalms and Proverbs to see what the wisdom literature teaches regarding anger. The *New American Standard Bible* uses the words "anger" and "angry" fifty-four times in these two books. "Anger" is used forty-five times while "angry" is used nine times. In the book of Psalms, which uses the words the most, only three times do the words refer to the anger of man. The rest of the time, anger is an emotion attached to God. Twice, anger refers to the anger of the author's enemies. It is important to note that these enemies are assumed to be wicked. The third use is found in Psalm 37:8, where David offers the exhortation to "cease from anger, and forsake wrath; Do not fret, it leads only to evildoing."

Do not miss the significance of this fact. Of the thirty-eight times Psalms uses either "anger" or "angry," only three times does the book of Psalms attach anger to man, what James would call "the anger of man." The first of these is Psalm 37:8 where the Psalmist commands "cease from anger." This is the same Psalm that says in verse four to "delight" in the Lord. In verse seven, the Psalmist says to "rest in the Lord." The commands to delight in the Lord, and rest in the Lord stand in contrast with the command to cease from anger. It seems that David is instructing the people of God that a man cannot restfully delight in God and be angry. This brings to mind Jesus' words in Matthew 6:24 that "no one can serve two masters."

The second instance of man's anger in the Psalms is 55:3. Notice who is angry. "Because of the voice of the enemy, because of the pressure of the wicked; for they bring down trouble upon me and in anger they bear a grudge against me." It is the voice of the enemy, the pressure of the wicked. Those who are angry are the enemies of David, the Lord's anointed. They are called the wicked—the wicked will all perish.[11] The characteristic of expressing anger is attributed to those who hate God. Surely it is not a trait commended to the people of God. It conforms to the New Testament usage of anger which attributes anger with the

---

[11] Psalms 1:6 "For the Lord knows the way of the righteous, but the way of the wicked will perish."

deeds of the flesh.

In Psalm 124:3,[12] a Psalm of ascents written by David, he again attributes anger to his enemies. It is those who stand against the Lord and His anointed, those mentioned in Psalm 2[13] demanding to be free from God's restrains, who express their anger. Anger, is an expression of judgment. God reserves judgment to Himself. He calls His people to leave room for His judgment, trusting Him to do what is right. When someone decides to judge another, being angry with them, that person has set his heart against God's redemptive purposes for the other person. God may yet speak life and bestow forgiveness to the one who was wrong. To be angry with them blocks the individual from seeking this ultimate good in the other person's life.

The book of Proverbs uses the words "anger" and "angry" fifteen times. Four times it refers to the anger of authorities— those whom God has appointed to dispense justice on the earth. Twice it speaks of avoiding another person's anger. The remaining nine uses speak of the anger of man. In every occasion, anger is viewed as negative, and being slow to anger as a good thing (14:29[14], 15:18[15], 16:32[16], 19:11[17]). Anger is connected to folly (12:16[18]), strife (15:18, 29:22[19]), and punishment (19:19[20]). Controlling one's anger requires great understanding (14:29), it pacifies contention (15:18) and is an expression of strength (16:32). Wise men leave anger behind and do not associate with those given to anger (22:24[21]). The virtue of being slow to anger is extolled throughout the book. This makes sense because God calls

---

[12] Psalms 124:3 "Then they would have swallowed us alive, when their anger was kindled against us..."

[13] Psalms 2:5 "Then He will speak to them in His anger and terrify them in His fury, saying..."

[14] Proverbs 14:29 "He who is slow to anger has great understanding, but he who is quick-tempered exalts folly."

[15] Proverbs 15:18 "A hot-tempered man stirs up strife, but the slow to anger calms a dispute."

[16] Proverbs 16:32 "He who is slow to anger is better than the mighty, and he who rules his spirit, than he who captures a city."

[17] Proverbs 19:11 "A man's discretion makes him slow to anger, and it is his glory to overlook a transgression."

[18] Proverbs 12:16 "A fool's anger is known at once, but a prudent man conceals dishonor."

[19] Proverbs 29:22 "An angry man stirs up strife,and a hot-tempered man abounds in transgression."

[20] Proverbs 19:19 "A man of great anger will bear the penalty, for if you rescue him, you will only have to do it again."

[21] Proverbs 22:24 "Do not associate with a man given to anger; or go with a hot-tempered man..."

Himself "slow to anger" at least nine different times in the Old Testament.

A brief study of anger in the Old Testament reveals the same conclusions that are drawn from the New Testament. The anger of man does not accomplish God's purposes but rather is an expression of folly. A common objection to this is, "But Jesus was angry." Where does the Bible says that Jesus was angry? A common assumption is that Jesus was angry when He drove the money changers out of the temple. While it is easy to attribute anger to Jesus in this instance, God attributes an entirely different motive to Jesus. God says that Jesus acted out of zeal, not anger. The New Testament does not say that He was angry in this instance. It is possible that He was angry; however, one cannot build an understanding of anger based on what is not in the Bible. Instead, honesty requires the student to consider what is in the Bible.

In only one instance (Mark 3:5) is Jesus said to be angry.

[1] He entered again into a synagogue; and a man was there whose hand was withered. [2] They were watching Him to see if He would heal him on the Sabbath, so that they might accuse Him. [3] He said to the man with the withered hand, "Get up and come forward!" [4] And He said to them, "Is it lawful to do good or to do harm on the Sabbath, to save a life or to kill?" But they kept silent. [5] After looking around at them with anger, grieved at their hardness of heart, He said to the man, "Stretch out your hand." And he stretched it out, and his hand was restored.

In this situation, Jesus is seated in the synagogue on the Sabbath and notices a man with a withered hand. The man was brought to the synagogue by the Pharisees in the expectation that Jesus would heal him and therefore violate the Sabbath restrictions on work. They would finally be able to disprove His claims of divine origin. Jesus sees the man's suffering (something the Pharisees missed as he was only a tool to them). Jesus is angered by the willingness of these men to use a man's suffering as a tool to accomplish such wickedness as condemning the Son of God. His love for this man fills Him with anger toward those who would so use him.

From this fact one can rightly conclude that there is a possibility of righteous anger. However, it is important to note that Jesus is perfect and incapable of sin. The rest of mankind is not. What is possible for God may in fact be beyond man's ability in his current sinful state. If one is to experience a righteous anger, it will be borne from a love for other people, as Jesus' was. It will not be about the individual feeling the anger. For example, a pastor was assisting a woman who was divorcing her husband for molesting their children. The husband petitioned the court to be granted the house. He would not be able to leave prison and live in the house, but he wanted to attack his wife once more by taking away her home. The pastor was filled with a righteous anger at such wickedness. There is a possibility of righteous anger, but such anger will always be an expression of love for another, and not a judgment for a personal wrong suffered.

With that being said, the profusion of warnings about anger and commands to remove all anger should cause one to be suspicious of his own anger when it rises in the heart. In fact, as will be discussed later, the presence of anger can be a clear indicator of faulty thinking and misplaced faith. If one's first expectation about anger is that it is wrong, the individual is more likely to recognize and alter his wrong thinking.

If people are to learn to control their anger, they must begin by accepting God's perspective that anger is ordinarily inappropriate for the Christian. In addition, they need to understand what role anger plays in their lives. Anger, like the other negative emotions, is a warning light. It tells a person that he is not thinking and believing truth. If one accepts that anger is wrong, he will more readily stop himself when he feels anger and take the steps to change.

Why do I get angry?
A person gets angry because she does not get what she wants. Is it as simple as that? Not completely, but it provides a

great starting point. An important insight that the two boys mentioned earlier provide is that each person is responsible for her own anger. It is common to say, "You make me so mad!" or "That is annoying." These statements reveal a flawed thinking. Those who say such things are convinced that certain situations or people are able to evoke anger from them. They think that some things are inherently angering, that no other response is possible. Such thoughts make them slaves to the whims of others.

Compare this perspective with 1 Corinthians 10:13, "No temptation has overtaken you but such as is common to man; and God is faithful, who will not allow you to be tempted beyond what you are able, but with the temptation will provide the way of escape also, that you may be able to endure it." This chapter has already demonstrated the scriptural teaching that ordinarily anger is sinful. 1 Corinthians 10:13 shows us that there is never a situation in which an individual must give in to temptation and sin. Therefore, the idea that some things are inherently angering cannot be true. There must be another choice in the midst of moments that are deemed frustrating.

Consider how Jesus dealt with disrespect and insults. If there was ever a time in which an individual was disrespected it was when the Roman guard abused Jesus before the crucifixion. Jesus, who deserved ultimate respect as the living God, was beaten, mocked and spat upon. These expressions of disrespect occurred just hours after He was betrayed with a kiss and abandoned by men in whom He had invested three years of His life. If ever a situation demanded an angry response it was this one. Even so, there is no hint in any of the records of the event that Jesus was angry. Instead, Jesus prays for those who abused Him, "Father, forgive them. They do not know what they are doing."[22]

When an honest observer sees Jesus absorb such disrespect and respond to it with total forgiveness, he should be in awe of true power. Every believer should want to experience that power in their life. Such power is available for the Christian. Consider

[22] Luke 23:34

15

Ephesians 3:20, "Now to Him who is able to do far more abundantly beyond all that we ask or think according to the power that works within us." God's people have that power. They can access it to overcome their own anger.

People get angry, in part, because they forget that they do not have to get angry. They willingly relinquish control of their lives to those who oppose them or to the situations that they face. The second factor in anger is a failure to get what is wanted. To say it a little more precisely, your anger stems from the belief that someone or something prevents you from getting what you believe you need.

James 4:1-2 asks, "What is the source of quarrels and conflicts among you? Is not the source your pleasures that wage war in your members? You lust and do not have; so you commit murder. You are envious and cannot obtain; so you fight and quarrel. You do not have because you do not ask." An individual's desires bring that person into conflict with others. He may think he needs someone to show him respect. When he does not get that respect, he will lash out in anger, passing judgment on the other person resulting in conflict.

Every person has an uncanny ability to confuse his proper desires with his needs. A woman may say things like, "I need my coffee in the morning," or, "I need at least eight hours of sleep each night." It is common to discount these statements as harmless exaggerations and yet what if they are actually accurate expressions of the heart. The move from "I need coffee" to "I need my husband to respect me" is far too easy to make. The problem is that both statements are false.

What do I need?
Man was created. To be created means that someone else created him. By the very fact of man's existence it can be deduced that man is dependent. The cosmological argument for God, as presented by Thomas Aquinas, considers the reality that all of life is in motion.

The first and more manifest way is the argument

from motion. It is certain, and evident to our senses, that in the world some things are in motion. Now whatever is in motion is put in motion by another, for nothing can be in motion except it is in potentiality to that towards which it is in motion; whereas a thing moves inasmuch as it is in act. For motion is nothing else than the reduction of something from potentiality to actuality. But nothing can be reduced from potentiality to actuality, except by something in a state of actuality. Thus that which is actually hot, as fire, makes wood, which is potentially hot, to be actually hot, and thereby moves and changes it. Now it is not possible that the same thing should be at once in actuality and potentiality in the same respect, but only in different respects. For what is actually hot cannot simultaneously be potentially hot; but it is simultaneously potentially cold. It is therefore impossible that in the same respect and in the same way a thing should be both mover and moved, i.e. that it should move itself. Therefore, whatever is in motion must be put in motion by another. If that by which it is put in motion be itself put in motion, then this also must needs be put in motion by another, and that by another again. But this cannot go on to infinity, because then there would be no first mover, and, consequently, no other mover; seeing that subsequent movers move only inasmuch as they are put in motion by the first mover; as the staff moves only because it is put in motion by the hand. Therefore it is necessary to arrive at a first mover, put in motion by no other; and his everyone understands to be God.[23]

Motion, as Aquinas uses it, means that things change. He points out that nothing moves without a force being applied to it. Think of inertia. An object at rest will remain at rest unless some

---

[23] Thomas Aquinas, *Summa Theologica* Part 1 Q. 2 http://www.ccel.org/ccel/aquinas/summa.pdf

force is applied to move it. An object in motion will continue in motion unless some force is applied to stop it. Since everything is in motion, in order to avoid an infinite regress, one must conclude an initial unmoved "first mover"; a truly independent being. That independent being must be God.

Thomas' argument posits the idea that God alone is independent. Man is dependent on God for his being. In addition, man continues to exist in a dependent relationship. Paul tells the Athenians that in God "We live and move and have our being" (Acts 17:28). Man depends on God for everything. It is this dependent reality of man's relationship to God that promotes prayer. People are to seek from the giver of all good things that which they need: God Himself. As He is the one who personally meets each man's needs, it can be concluded that it is not the gift, but the giver that each man truly needs. If the gift exists without the giver, man will still perish. However, if the giver exists without the gift, man will still have his needs met by the giver.

Consider what may be the most important phrase in the world, "but God." These two words instruct the mind that God is all that each person needs. This phrase is used forty-one times in the NASB. Consider a few of the uses.

Noah is on a boat with his family and two of every kind of animal. God has just blotted out all life from the face of the earth with a flood and it has been raining for 150 days. As Noah looks out upon a world covered in water, what must have passed through his mind? Can you imagine the uncertainty about the future? In the midst of such uncertainty, Genesis 8:1 says, "**But God** remembered Noah..." But God changed everything. Joseph is reunited with his brothers, who threw him into a pit and sold him into slavery. The brothers are terrified of Joseph because their father has just died. They stand before Joseph, afraid that he will now bring retribution to them, but consider Joseph's words from Genesis 50:20, "you meant it for evil **but God** meant it for good." In 1 Samuel 23:14, as Saul is hunting for David every day Samuel records these words of hope; "**but God** did not deliver him into his hand." God does not allow Saul to capture David. In Mark 2:7, the Pharisees seek to condemn Jesus for forgiving a lame man. They say, "Who can forgive sins **but God** alone?" The Pharisees understood a significant idea. Man is sinful. He deserves eternal destruction. Man is truly in a helpless situation, but God can forgive. Paul iterates this same concept in Ephesians 2:1-3. He explains that he and the Ephesians were all dead in their sins and without hope. Then in Ephesians 2:4-5 he says, "**But God** being rich in mercy because of His great love with which He loved us, made us alive together with Christ..."

The words "but God" are helpful reminders that God is all that any person really needs. People frequently talk about needing air and food and water. What happens if they lack these? They will die. Is that the end? No! If a person dies, and they have a right relationship with God, they enter into bliss. In addition to this it must remembered that God is capable of sustaining life even without air, food or water. This is what Paul meant when He said in Romans 8:31, "What then shall we say to these things? If God is for us, who is against us?" All you need is God. And He has given you all that you need. Not only do you need God, but He is actively providing those needs. If you are to ever remove anger from your life, you must fill your mind with this truth and order your life consistent with it. You do not need coffee, respect from your spouse or financial security.

Try this exercise to begin to discipline your mind with this truth. Each day for the next week, keep a journal of each time that you get angry. Take time to meditate on this anger and write down the events that led to your anger. Ask yourself what you really wanted in this situation. Now, write a sentence that explains your frustration and then insert the words, "but God..." Your entry may read something like this: "Yesterday we got a notice of a bounced check. My wife accused me of mismanaging our finances. I really want her to respect me, *but God* knows I made a mistake and He forgives me. He also gives me the ability to do a better job." This exercise can help you put this truth into practice.

This brief study of the topic of anger from the Bible provides a useful tool to battle anger. First, the Scriptures demonstrate that anger is not an innocuous emotion. Instead, in man it is ordinarily a sinful response to situations and people who fail to act as desired. Second, the Bible teaches that a person controls his own emotions. One does not have to get angry. People can choose instead to respond in love, like Jesus. This response is only possible if we remember that God is all that we need. Therefore, each one of us can and must place our faith in His love for us.

After Alan put the milk into the fridge, he slammed the door. As he did, a drawing that Debbie had made in Sunday school fell to the floor. Alan looked at it before he replaced it on the refrigerator door. It had a rainbow, a cross and the words, "God loves me" written on it. The simple message touched Alan's angry heart. He had snapped at Debbie during dinner. He had not shown her God's love tonight. Then he thought about why he was so mad. "Out of the mouths of babes..." he thought. Alan stopped and prayed quietly, "Father, thanks for all of the ways you show me your love. Thanks for my beautiful daughter. Thanks for Sally. She really is great. Will you help me to love her for You. Amen!" With those words, Alan felt a new resolve to reach out to his wife and show her how much Jesus cares about her.

2 MY NEEDS

I said to the Lord, "Thou art my Lord;
I have no good besides Thee."
Psalm 16:2

Justin settled into his seat on the plane bound for Africa. This was his first mission trip. The days leading up to the trip had been busy. Last minute shopping, shots, and getting the bills paid so that Helen would not have to worry about it. He and Helen had been married for three years. They joined the Crestdale Community Church last year. When Pastor Wallace mentioned that the Church would take a group to Africa, Justin was excited. This is just what he needed.

Things at home had been growing tense. He and Helen were both working full time. Helen was moving up in her company. She worked a lot of extra hours. They both attended accountability groups at Crestdale Church. Justin met with the men for breakfast on Tuesdays and Helen met with the women on Thursday evenings. With their work and Church schedule, Justin and Helen did not get to spend much time talking. He felt they were growing apart. With this sense of distance, they were fussing at each other more and more. Justin was beginning to worry about their future.

Work was not much better. Justin was assigned to a project that required about 70 hours a week. He had to make three trips to Washington in the last two months. His dream was to move up in this company. However, lately, it seemed he was invisible. When special opportunities came up, he was overlooked. He did not want to be a squeaky wheel, but how else could he get noticed?

The leader of the men's breakfast group had told Justin that the solution might be to get outside of himself. If he found some way to serve other people, he would find greater happiness. Then Pastor Wallace announced this mission trip to Africa.

Pastor Wallace had challenged all of the team members to pray about the trip. He wanted them to ask God to work in their lives in a powerful way during the trip. Justin remembered this instruction and began to pray.

"Lord, I really would like you to do something remarkable in my life this next week. I cannot imagine what it might be. Here I am."

At this point, Justin's mind was suddenly filled with the problems back home. He prayed again. "I guess what I really need is for you to help Helen. She seems so distant from me lately. We don't talk as much as we used to and I wonder if she loves me. I cannot bear the idea that this is what life has in store for us. I need her to be closer to me. What good is it to be married if your wife doesn't love you? God, give her a greater love for me. Help her love me like a wife should her husband. Surely, that will please You.

"I also need you to help at my work. I am so discouraged. I thought it would be so easy to move up. I just needed to work hard and then people would see my value to the company. It is starting to feel so meaningless. My boss doesn't notice how hard I work. Other people are advancing and I still sit in my same cubicle doing the same thing I have done for the last five years. It feels so unfair. God, I really need a better job. Will you please help? I ask this in Jesus' name, Amen."

With this prayer, Justin fell asleep. He was going to Africa.

Four days later, a van carrying Justin, Pastor Wallace, and five other missionaries pulled up to the prison compound. The team was going to conduct a worship service at the local prison. As they drove into the compound, Justin noticed that there were no trees. The ground was just dirt, trampled by thousands of feet for many years. Dust rose around a small group of prisoners playing soccer. The heat of the day struck Justin as he exited the van. "It must be 100 degrees out here."

The group of men entered the fenced area where they met a guard with a three foot rubber hose. He pointed to the small concrete area with a roof and no walls. Men from all over the prison yard began to walk toward the concrete slab. Each man was smiling with those huge disarming African smiles. One of the men began to sing. The others joined in response to his words. Soon they were clapping, dancing and singing praise to Jesus. Justin could not understand all of the words. Occasionally, he could hear "Jehovah" or "Jesus" coming from the voices around him. He was deeply moved to see such love for God in a place like this. During the service the men sat in rapt attention as Pastor Wallace taught them from the Scriptures. One of the prisoners translated while the rest listened and offered an occasional "Amen!"

After the service, a man named Peter came up to Justin and said, "Thank you for coming to us." Peter shared that he had been in the prison for seven years. He had not gone to trial because the police lost his file. He hoped that one day he would be free. His wife brought him clothes twice a year. He ate corn meal mush every day. When his wife came he would get some meat. Peter went on to explain his role in the prison. He helped with the Church. He preached once a month and helped tell other prisoners about Jesus. While he had been in prison, God had brought ten other prisoners to salvation. He smiled and said, "God is so good!"

God Plus

So what do people actually need? The last chapter mentioned that all man needs is God. The way this is usually

interpreted is that people need God to save them. People need God
to provide food, water, and shelter. A husband needs God to help
his wife respect him; provide a job that pays the bills, children that
obey, and an adequate retirement plan. Such an interpretation is
simply a new way of stating the old error that people need
something more than God. Most people think they need Jesus
most, but they also need a lot of other things. People need Jesus
plus. "Jesus plus" is the idea to which many have committed their
lives.

This conviction is strengthened by the way that many
people interpret much of Scripture. How often have well-meaning
preachers and teachers exhorted their congregations to make God
their highest priority? Gayle Sayers, the star running back for the
Chicago Bears, wrote the book *I Am Third,* which inspired the
movie *Brian's Song.* In this book Sayers propounds a set of
priorities that at first glance seem reasonable: God, family, and
then me. It would appear that God, family, and then me is the right
set of priorities in the Christian life. This thinking may be
supported by a cursory reading of Exodus 20:3, "You shall have no
other gods before me." This seems to indicate that God wants first
place in people's lives. It is believed that as long as none of the
other things become more important than God, everything is right.

A closer look at the Scripture provides a different
perspective. The Hebrew word translated as "before me" in
Exodus 20:3 is עַל־פָּנָיַ which literally means "before my face." It
does not speak of priorities at all. In English, the word "before" is
somewhat ambiguous. It is often used to mean a position in line—
such as, "That person was here *before* me." It is also used to
mean "in the presence of someone." We say that a criminal stands
"*before*" the judge. In this context, the word "before" means "in
the presence and under the full attention" of the judge. God
commands His people to have no other gods as they stand in His
presence.

As God inspects the lives of His people, He wants to find
that He is their only God. He will not share his people with other
gods. He is a jealous God.[24] Jesus makes this same point in

Matthew 6:24, "No one can serve two masters; for either he will hate the one and love the other, or he will hold to one and despise the other. You cannot serve God and mammon." God is not pleased with being the most important thing in one's life. He wants to be the only thing.

What constitutes another god in my life? It is so easy to assert that one has no other gods, but Scripture seems to indicate that idolatry is a common problem. Consider 2 Kings 17:35, "with whom the Lord made a covenant and commanded them, saying, 'You shall not fear other gods, nor bow down yourselves to them nor serve them nor sacrifice to them.'" God describes the actions which constitute idolatry. He forbids his people to "fear" other gods. "The fear of the Lord is the beginning of wisdom"[25] but to fear anything else is to lack trust. Ask yourself, "What am I afraid of losing?" The answer to this question may show you some other gods lurking in the recesses of your heart. When Daniel found himself in a position to risk losing his relationship with God by praying only to Nebuchadnezzar's idol or losing his life, he chose to protect his relationship with God. The Lord was his only god.

Secondly, God's people are not to "bow down" to other gods. One bows down to something that is viewed as superior. What makes you feel inferior? The only opinion of you that matters is God's. One should only bow to the Lord. This is demonstrated by the angelic messenger to whom John bows down in the book of Revelation. He is told, "Do not do that; I am a fellow servant..."[26] Whatever makes me feel inferior may be my god.

2 Kings continues to describe idolatry by saying, "nor serve them." This description has to do with the person one treats as his lord. It requires the listener to ask, "Whom do you obey?" Yes, believers are to obey authorities in their life—according to the fifth commandment—but why obey them? Obedience to the civil authority is an obedience first offered to God. When the authority

---

[24] Exodus 20:5 "You shall not worship them or serve them; for I, the Lord your God, am a jealous God..."
[25] Proverbs 1:7
[26] Revelation 19:10, 22:9.

commands something inconsistent with God's will, the conscientious follower of Christ must disobey (Daniel 1, 3, and 6).

Finally, the people of God are instructed not to "sacrifice to them." For what will one sacrifice his family, income, or integrity? This may be his god. Recently a pastor of a very large church was deposed for stealing prescription drugs from friends to feed his habit. The relief of pain led this man to set aside a career he had spent years building. Another man lost his wife and family because of an affair with a co-worker. He had been married for twenty years, but when the opportunity to have an illicit relationship presented itself, he obeyed his lust instead of submitting to the command of Christ. Many idols command the believer to follow. Whom will you obey?

Think about Matthew 5:8 in light of this idea of God's exclusive claim on His people's lives. "Blessed are the pure in heart; for they shall see God." Pure water is water without anything in it except water. Pure gold possesses nothing but gold. What then is a pure heart? A pure heart is one that has the true God as its single point of focus. It is for this that man was created in the first place. The person who has a heart singularly committed to Jesus will see God. Throughout Scripture, God's invites his people to make Him their everything. Asaph discovered this truth and penned the words found in Psalm 73:25, "Whom have I in heaven but You? And besides You I desire nothing on earth."

To live as though God is all that one needs is a terrifying act. In it the believer is stripped of everything: power, merit, friends, and even family. Jesus said in Luke 14:26, "If anyone comes to Me, and does not hate his own father and mother and wife and children and brothers and sisters, yes, and even his own life, he cannot be My disciple." The Christian life requires that an individual stand alone before God. No one and nothing can mediate except the Lord Jesus. In this state, one is fully at His mercy. This is where salvation dwells.

The belief that I need "God plus..." demonstrates a commitment to living comfortably here on this earth. People are committed to it because they believe they need a comfortable life here on earth. There might be a heaven, and it might be pretty nice. But what if heaven does not exist? Does one really want to risk everything on an archaic idea of an afterlife filled with bliss? After all, look at all of the godly people around who are living the good life here and now and who expect glory too.

While in Seminary, One of my professors once told a story about one of his students. One day the professor told his class that money makes no difference to God. Rich and poor were all the same to Him. One student sought clarification, "You mean it doesn't matter if we are rich or poor?"

"That's right."

"Then I'll take rich."

The professor smiled. "You got me there. I was wrong. God never warns about the danger of poverty. He does say it is easier for a camel to fit through the eye of a needle than for a rich man to enter heaven. So you see, it is better to be poor." The student's initial response seems reasonable. People think they can choose just Jesus or Jesus plus the "good life." Not surprisingly, they choose the plus. But God will have none of it. He knows that to seek Him plus other things is to seek less than Him; in the same way that to choose water plus dirt is less than just water. The "plus" is an impurity that will keep one from seeing God. He wants the very best for His people and the very best is a pure heart, a heart exclusively devoted to Him.

One's conviction in this area can be deeply strengthened by visiting third world countries. In each of these areas of deep poverty, one comes face to face with the fact that if people need God plus the accoutrements of a comfortable life, then God is failing most people on this planet. He is simply not providing for millions of people even though many of them are Christians. What is striking, particularly in Africa, is how these believers do not expect God to make them wealthy or even comfortable. They live with the reality that they are a mosquito bite away from a painful death. Most of them though are looking for something more. This world is not their home, and they know it. Therefore, they pray not for safety but for faithfulness.

My Needs: Love

What needs are met in God alone? To answer that question, look at Genesis 2:7. "Then the Lord God formed man of dust from the ground, and breathed into his nostrils the breath of life; and man became a living being." Here God reveals the specific way in which He created man. Sometimes people assume God said, "Let there be man." And there was man. And God saw that man was good. Genesis 2 gives a much more intimate view of this miraculous event. God formed the man out of dust and then placed the breath of life into him. God could have simply spoken, and man would have become a living being. He could have said, "I give you the breath of life." Instead, the Scripture specifically records that God Almighty placed His face upon Adam's face and sent His own breath into the man's nostrils.

This is similar to rescue breathing on an infant. The rescuer covers the child's mouth and nose and sends his living breath into the child. God the Father granted life to man in much the same way. Imagine Adam's first thoughts as life begins to pulse through his body. Adam opens his eyes and sees the face of his creator. He is aware that these eyes staring into his are filled with deep love for him. He is completely accepted in this place, inches from the lips of the one who spoke all creation into existence. He knows above all else that living involves being in the face of God, finding the perfect acceptance which he now sees in the face of his Maker. He must continually remain so close to God that he draws all of his life from God's presence. Adam knew that he needed an intimate relationship of love with God or he would cease to exist.

Each of Adam's descendants shares this deep need for unconditional acceptance. Every baby is born with the expectation of being accepted and loved. The newborn has no interest or ability to earn acceptance, but if it is withheld, the child will perish. As we grow, this cruel, sin-cursed world teaches us that there is no free lunch. To be accepted as an adult we cannot just cry when we are hungry or tired. We cannot expect others to bring us whatever we want. One needs to be nice to people in order to be liked. Unconditional acceptance is absent from people's lives, but they still need it. Our needs will never be met by those who also need the same unconditional acceptance. Everyone is needy, and when each person seeks his needs to be met by those who are themselves empty, only dissatisfaction can occur. This is why everyone must seek God alone to meet their needs.

Notice how God addresses man's need of His love throughout Scripture. The oft repeated clause, "I will be your God, and you will be my people" shows the heart of God for a relationship with man.[27] He assures His people of His love. Deuteronomy 7:7-9 says,

> The Lord did not set His love on you nor choose you because you were more in number than any of the peoples, for you were the fewest of all peoples, but because the Lord loved you and kept the oath which He swore to your forefathers, the Lord brought you out by a mighty hand and redeemed you from the house of slavery, from the hand of Pharaoh king of Egypt. Know therefore that the Lord your God, He is God, the faithful God, who keeps His covenant and His lovingkindness to a thousandth generation with those who love Him and keep His commandments;

He reiterates this truth in passages like Hosea, where He illustrates His love for His people through a prophet who marries a harlot and remains faithful to her, unwilling to give her up. He speaks of His love in Jeremiah 31:3 when He says, "I have loved you with an everlasting love; Therefore I have drawn you with lovingkindness." John 3:16 reveals the purpose of the incarnation, "For God so loved the world." In Ephesians 2:4-5, God explains His motivation in saving His people, "But God, being rich in mercy, because of the great love with which He loved us..." God knows man's need to be loved by Him, and He continually reminds His people of His love.

---

[27] Genesis 17:7; Exodus 19:5; Jeremiah 30:22; Ezekiel 36:28; 1 Peter 2:9; Revelation 21:7

You see, man was not created to need people. Adam was created with the need for God's unconditional love and acceptance. Each person has this same need. Everyone thirsts for God. Augustine put it this way, "Thou hast made us for Thyself, O Lord,

and our hearts are restless until they rest in Thee."[28] This need is so powerful that men spend their entire lives trying to quench it. Some find the wellspring and drink deeply of the love of Jesus. Others, even Christians, never quite find the source of satisfaction that they need until they see Him face to face. Most people go from relationship to relationship hoping that this one will finally quench the awful burning in their soul.

Value

In addition to unconditional acceptance, people all need purpose. Turn your attention to Genesis 1:28. "And God blessed them; and God said to them, 'Be fruitful and multiply, and fill the earth, and subdue it; and rule over the fish of the sea and over the birds of the sky, and over every living thing that moves on the earth.'" God created Adam and Eve in His own image and then called them to work. The work that He gave them was consistent with whom God had made them to be. Their dignity was not found in the task they were given, but in who they were as unique reflections of God.   This uniqueness, when joined with the opportunity to express it within the context of their task, gave great purpose to their lives. Even Jesus knew that He had a purpose. He said, "The Son of man did not come to be served but to serve" and "the Son of man came to seek and to save that which is lost." Without a purpose, people cease to function as image-bearers of God.

One's purpose is inseparably tied to the concept of God's image. What does it mean to be created in the image of God? At the central core of one's being a person is made to uniquely reveal something of God. This is a part of what the Westminster Divines meant when they declared that man's chief end is to glorify God[29].

---

[28] St. Augustine, *The Nicene and Post-Nicene Fathers Volume One* (William B. Eerdmans Publishing Company, Grand Rapids 1983) 45

That which man is created to do, the greatest possible goal of one's existence is to glorify God. To glorify God means simply to reflect the magnificent glory that God has in Himself.

Psalm 19:1 says that all of creation reveals God, declaring His glory. "The heavens are telling of the glory of God; and their expanse is declaring the work of His hands." If a piece of granite somehow glorifies God by being fully granite, and a wave on the ocean glorifies God by rolling across the sea according to God's intention, how much more is an individual human being able to demonstrate God's glory by being precisely the individual whom God intended him to be.

In Psalm 139, David reflects on God's activity in his life. He records his meditation concerning God's personal involvement in his life. In verses 13-16 he writes:

For Thou didst form my inward parts;
Thou didst weave me in my mother's womb.
I will give thanks to Thee, for I am fearfully and
wonderfully made;
Wonderful are Thy works,
And my soul knows it very well.
My frame was not hidden from Thee,
When I was made in secret,
And skillfully wrought in the depths of the earth.
Thine eyes have seen my unformed substance;
And in Thy book they were all written,
The days that were ordained for me,
When as yet there was not one of them.

Notice that David prays in the first person singular. He does not say "us" or "we" but "I," "me," and "my." In this way, God reveals that He is active in the formation of each individual, not just the human race in general. David is not speaking of the general concept of creation, acknowledging that God made Adam, and then left people alone to make their own offspring. Instead,

---

[29] Westminster Shorter Catechism #1 "What is the chief end of man?" Answer "The chief end of man is to glorify God and enjoy Him forever."

31

God shows that He is active in the formation of every single individual who ever lives. His involvement is not simply a matter of knowledge about the person but rather a purposeful design and constant care by which each person is made to uniquely show something of God to the watching universe.

Just as David was given the unique qualities that made him the sweet psalmist of Israel, the man after God's own heart, God has designed you, me, your family, and the homeless man downtown to be a means of displaying Himself to all of creation. One's purpose then is not found in what he does but in who he is and how he does his work. One's work is not what gives him significance; instead the person gives their work significance. One's work is simply the environment in which the individual reveals God.

God does not withdraw His hand once a person is born. Instead He continues to be actively involved in directing men's lives. He continues to form them through the events of their lives. Read James 1:2-4, "Consider it all joy, my brethren, when you encounter various trials, knowing that the testing of your faith produces endurance. And let endurance have its perfect result, so that you may be perfect and complete, lacking in nothing." Romans 5:3-5 says,

> And not only this, but we also exult in our tribulations, knowing that tribulation brings about perseverance; and perseverance, proven character; and proven character, hope; and hope does not disappoint, because the love of God has been poured out within our hearts through the Holy Spirit who was given to us.

In both of these passages the authors reveal that trials have purpose. They produce endurance which shapes people's lives. Each person that we meet and every situation that we face provides opportunities to learn who we are in God's eyes and how we might better reflect Him. Each of us is a tool in God's hand to shape people, to refine them to more accurately display that part of God they were created to reveal.

The question, "Who am I?" is only answered in relation to God. God's perspective of who you are is what defines you. He not only sees who you are, but by His power He declares who you are. He is your maker. Victor Hugo gave the world some marvelous characters through his novels. In *Les Miserables* he introduced Jean Valjean, a convict living always on the run from the law. Valjean's story has been put to music in the Broadway production based on Hugo's work. A common theme for Valjean through the play is "Who am I?" In one scene Valjean is wrestling with a decision. The answer to his dilemma is found by answering the haunting question, "Who am I?" He sings, "My soul belongs to God I know. I made that bargain long ago. Who am I?" Central to Valjean's understanding of who he is, is his relationship to God.

What does God think of you? Take a personal inventory during a time alone with God. Ask Him, "Who am I?" Listen. What values has God given to you that beautifully reflect Him? What abilities has He given you that reveal something of Him? What weaknesses do you possess that lead you to rely on Him? How do you hope to impact the people around you? In what specific ways would you like people to be more like Jesus after being around you?

To understand this question, think about your funeral. Stephen Covey, in his book *7 Habits of Highly Successful People* suggests that people can develop objectives for the type of character they wish to build by imagining what they want their family, friends, coworkers, and members of their church to say about them at their funeral. If a line of people stood to share how you influenced their lives, what would you want them to say? This exercise can bring into clearer focus this concept of finding one's real worth in being the person God has made you to be. It leads you to think truth about yourself. That is to say, you will then think what God thinks about you.

The German pastor and theologian, Dietrich Bonhoeffer meditated on this thought while he was in a Nazi prison.

Bonhoefer was imprisoned after he was involved in a plot to assassinate Hitler. He was eventually hanged for his crimes just days before his prison was liberated. He penned one of the most moving poems ever written.

Who Am I
By Dietrich Bonhoeffer

Who am I ? They often tell me,
I step out from my cell
Composed, contented and sure,
Like a lord from his manor.

Who am I ? They often tell me,
I speak with my jailers
Frankly, familiar and firm,
As though I was in command.

Who am I ? They also tell me,
I bear the days of hardship,
Unconcerned, amused and proud,
Like one who usually wins.

Am I really what others tell me?
Or am I only what I myself know of me?
Troubled, homesick, ill, like a bird in a cage,
Gasping for breath, as though one strangled me,
Hungering for colors, for flowers, for songs of birds,
Thirsting for kind words, for human company,

Quivering with anger at despotism and petty insults,
Anxiously waiting for great events,
Helplessly worrying about friends far away,
Empty and tired of praying, thinking, of working,
Exhausted and ready to bid farewell to it all.

Who am I? This or the other?
Am I then this today and the other tomorrow?
Am I both at the same time? In public, a hypocrite

And by myself a contemptible, whining weakling?
Or am I to myself, like a beaten army,
Flying in disorder from a victory already won?

Who am I? Lonely questions mock me.
Who I really am, you know me,
I am Thine, O God![30]

Truth

Jesus made an important statement in John 8:32, "And you shall know the truth, and the truth shall make you free." Clearly Jesus is speaking of Himself as truth and yet His statement is far deeper. The truth always sets free. Truth sets the young math student free from continual errors in calculations. Truth allows people to be free from the errors of history, enabling them to not repeat them. The truth of one's sin, coupled with the truth of Jesus' work at Calvary, sets a person free to walk in newness of life. The truth of who you are in the eyes of God sets you free to more accurately reflect Him through your life.

Truth can be defined as "God's perspective." This is more than the assertion that God always sees what is real. Jesus called himself, "the truth." This God is the one true God. He defines truth. Truth is unchanging, and it continually demands man's conformity. People conform to the truth of gravity every time they place their spoon underneath their soup. They conform to the truth of inertia every time they apply their brakes before they get to the intersection. The truth of God's perspective of who you really are is no different. Success demands that people conform to truth, so that they may most effectively bring glory to God.

Non-Christians refuse to acknowledge the truth that they are dead in their sin and separated from God. They do not submit to the truth that reconciliation with God is only possible through Jesus. Therefore, non-Christians fail to fully reflect God in this world. They are trapped in bondage to falsehood. If they will submit themselves to the truth, the truth will set them free.

---

[30] Dietrich Bonhoeffer, *Prison Poems. (, Grand Rapids,Zondervan 1999) 43-44*

A part of the struggle in this world is that lies are all around. The pressure to conform to untruth is a continual temptation. Friends want you to be a certain type of person. Your parents expect you to behave in a particular fashion. The culture influences people, as does the educational system, place of employment, and a thousand other forces. With all of these voices it is hard to know which ones to trust. Who is speaking God's perspective? That is the voice one must hear and follow. As people learn to hear God and ignore all other voices, they are set free to know and accomplish their purpose in life. One discovers who God sees when He looks at them. They learn how they can best express themselves to most fully reveal the greatness of their God. The only place in which one's need for purpose is met is in an intimate relationship with God.

God has honored mankind by allowing people to speak His words to one another. You can be the voice of God in other people's lives. Just as a person needs to spend time alone with God to know who he is, you can also seek His face to really get to know those around you. This does not mean that God will give you any special revelation of your friend's heart. Instead, God will help you to see God in the values other have, the struggles they face, and the hope that drives them. If you will seek God's face while you are with other people, you can grow in your ability to see who they really are.

Consider what God has said about His people. Believers are, in one sense, defined as those who believe. This is pretty obvious, and yet too often people expect other Christians to not believe. Christians are called saints because the imputed righteousness of Jesus is their possession. 2 Corinthians 5:17 says, "Therefore if anyone is in Christ, he is a new creature; the old things have passed away; behold new thing have come." The Christian is a new creature who is no longer dead to sin (Ephesians 2:4-5[31]) who no longer lives according to the flesh (Romans 8:9-11[32])

[31] Ephesians 2:4-5 4 "But God, being rich in mercy, because of His great love with which He loved us, 5 even when we were dead in our transgressions, made us alive together with Christ (by grace you have been saved)..."
[32] Romans 8:9-11" However, you are not in the flesh but in the Spirit, if indeed the Spirit of God dwells in you. But if anyone does not have the Spirit of Christ, he does not belong to Him. 10 If

who is empowered to resist temptation (1 Corinthians 10:13[33]). The Christian loves Jesus and wants, by the power of the Spirit, to honor Him with his life. All believers have the power to remind one another of this reality and thereby invite each other to live up to the truth of their place in Jesus Christ. What an honor God has given His people to speak truth, knowing that the truth will set people free!

Summary

What then do people need? They need to be unconditionally loved and accepted by the true and living God. They need a purpose for living that comes only from the One who is truth. They need God and only God. Asaph came to that realization in Psalm 73:25. Asaph struggled with the apparent injustice in the world. He saw that walking with God did not provide him with the stuff that he assumed brought happiness. He nearly fell until he entered the sanctuary of God and gained God's perspective. His conclusion is worthy of directing the Christian's entire life. "Whom have I in heaven but You? And besides You I desire nothing on earth." Man's needs are only met in a relationship with God. In one's relationship with God, all of his needs are met. May every man then seek Him alone!

Back on the plane, Justin reflected on what he had experienced in Africa. "God, You are good. You love me so very much. Seeing the contentment of the African Christians was powerful. They have nothing compared to me, but they know that all they really need is You. I am sorry that I am not satisfied with You. I spend so much of my time trying to get other people to respect me. I am frustrated that Helen doesn't love me more and yet I rarely think about how I can love her better. I am ready to rest in Your love. Will You help me to show Helen how much You love her? Will you help me to lead her to You? Father, I want to

---

Christ is in you, though the body is dead because of sin, yet the spirit is alive because of righteousness. [11] But if the Spirit of Him who raised Jesus from the dead dwells in you, He who raised Christ Jesus from the dead will also give life to your mortal bodies through His Spirit who dwells in you."

[33] 1 Corinthians 10:13 "No temptation has overtaken you but such as is common to man; and God is faithful, who will not allow you to be tempted beyond what you are able, but with the temptation will provide the way of escape also, so that you will be able to endure it."

be Your man at work. All that I am is by Your design. I want to be faithful in my call, just like Peter. You put him in a prison and he doesn't complain. He has found ways to serve You even behind bars. I want to serve You at my job. Help me to see how. I love You Lord! Thanks."

3 The Heart

And you will seek Me and find Me,
when you search for Me with all your heart.
Jeremiah 29:13

Some people are afraid to work on an engine. Whether the engine is in a car or a lawn mower, they get nervous at the prospect of working on an engine. Often times that reticence is tied to ignorance. They simply do not know how a combustion engine works. They do not know what its parts are or what they do. This ignorance leaves them unwilling to try to repair an engine.

A similar ignorance often leaves God's people in a state of disrepair. Many Christians, and even ministers, do not really understand how God has designed the heart. Christians easily repeat the words, "Love the Lord with all your heart" while not really knowing what the heart is. We cannot articulate its parts and we do not really grasp how each part works. Therefore, when faced with a significant struggle in our own life or in the life of a friend, we do not know how to bring real change. Those who are aware of their ignorance refer the struggling friend to a professional who may or may not know how to help.

It is good for someone who is ignorant of the workings of an internal combustion engine to let someone else work on their car. One could do some real damage if he tried to repair an engine while remaining ignorant of its proper working. In the same way, some Christians try to help people when they themselves do not know how the heart works. They offer counsel to hurting people but their advice is based on an inadequate understanding of how God has made man. With this errant perspective, their counsel is doomed to failure. This leaves many Christians with the conclusion that counseling is of no use. They continue in their struggles, never finding the relief that God provides.

Ephesians 4:14-16 tells us:

As a result, we are no longer to be children, tossed here and there by waves, and carried about by every wind of doctrine, by the trickery of men, by craftiness in deceitful scheming; but speaking the truth in love, we are to grow up in all aspects into Him, who is the head, even Christ, from whom the whole body, being fitted and held together by that which every joint supplies, according to the proper working of each individual part, causes the growth of the body for the building up of itself in love.

When God's people speak the truth in love, Christians are empowered to stand firm and affect the world as salt and light. The testimony of Holy Scripture and the experience of many Christians, whose lives have been transformed, proclaim the need to understand how God has made man. With understanding of what the Bible says about the heart will come a greater ability to impact this world.

The Heart

Proverbs 4:23 says, "Watch over your heart with all diligence, for from it flow the springs of life." Notice how important the heart is to God. He says, from it flow "springs of life," literally "the flowing of life." According to *The Theological Wordbook of the Old Testament* the word translated as "springs" comes from a root meaning "to go out." The idea of a spring is that the spring is where the water goes out of the earth. The heart is the spring from which life flows. Thus, it is of great importance to guard our hearts. The *Keil and Delitzsch Commentary on the Old Testament* says, "before all that one has to guard...guard it [the heart] as the most precious of possessions committed to thy trust."

It is common to posit a difference between the mind and the heart. Sometimes this distinction is made in order to emphasize the need to believe the Scriptures. At other times it serves to engage the emotions. While the goal may be noble, the language is inconsistent with the Bible's teaching about the heart. The Scripture refers to the heart as man's mind, will, and emotions. It may refer to any one of these individually or any combination of the three.

In John 16:22, Jesus says to His disciples, "Therefore you too now have sorrow; but I will see you again, and *your heart will rejoice*, and no one takes your joy away from you." Jesus says that the emotion of joy occurs in the heart. Psalm 19:8 reads, "The precepts of the Lord are right, rejoicing the heart..." Again it is the heart that experiences joy. Because the Lord is with him, David's heart is glad in Psalm 16:9[34]. The king noticed Nehemiah's sadness of heart in Nehemiah 2:2[35]. In Romans 9:2 Paul describes the grief in his heart concerning the lostness of his countrymen[36]. The Bible places the emotions firmly in the arena of the heart.

The heart is also the place where the will resides. The Bible uses the phrase "hardened heart" nineteen times. 1 Samuel 6:6 says, "Why then do you harden your hearts as the Egyptians and Pharaoh hardened their hearts? When He had severely dealt with them, did they not allow the people to go, and they departed?" Pharaoh hardened his heart when he refused to allow Israel to leave Egypt. Pharaoh saw the signs demonstrating God's power and yet he chose to resist God. This purposeful choice is called a hardened heart. Contrast the hardened heart of Pharaoh with David, the man after God's own heart. In Psalm 119:112, "I have inclined my heart to perform Thy statutes forever, even to the end." David inclines his heart to obedience. He makes the choice

---

[34] Psalms 16:9 "Therefore my heart is glad and my glory rejoices; my flesh also will dwell securely."
[35] Nehemiah 2:2 "So the king said to me, "Why is your face sad though you are not sick? This is nothing but sadness of heart." Then I was very much afraid."
[36] Romans 9:2 "that I have great sorrow and unceasing grief in my heart."

to obey God. That choice is an act of his heart. The heart involves both the emotions and the will.

The heart also refers to the mind. Luke 9:47 says, "But Jesus, knowing what they were thinking in their heart..." God brought the flood upon the world because He saw that in man, "every intent of the thoughts of his heart was only evil continually" (Genesis 6:5). In Psalm 119:11[37], David hides God's word in his heart so that he will not sin against God. It is common to use this same imagery when speaking of knowing something by heart. It means to memorize something.

These passages demonstrate that the Bible places the mind, the will, and the emotions in the realm of the heart. The greatest commandment, which is found in Deuteronomy 6:5, says, "You shall love the LORD your God with all your heart and with all your soul and with all your might." Mind, will, and emotions united in exclusive love for God is the greatest objective of man's existence. This whole-hearted love is what *The Train* is intended to promote.

The Mind

First consider the mind. Ayn Rand pointed out the importance of the mind and its relationship to man's will in her epic novel, *Atlas Shrugged*.

Man's mind is his basic tool of survival. Life is given to him, survival is not. His body is given to him, its sustenance is not. His mind is given to him, its content is not. To remain alive, he must act, and before he can act he must know the nature and purpose of his action. He cannot obtain his food without a knowledge of food and of the way to obtain it. He cannot dig a ditch— or build a cyclotron— without a knowledge of his aim and of the means to achieve it. To remain alive, he must think.

[37] Psalms 119:11 "Your word I have treasured in my heart, that I may not sin against You."

But to think is an act of choice. The key to what you so recklessly call 'human nature,' the open secret you live with, yet dread to name , is the fact that man is a being of volitional consciousness. Reason does not work automatically; thinking is not a mechanical process; the connections of logic are not made by instinct. The function of your stomach, lungs or heart is automatic; the function of your mind is not. In any hour and issue of your life, you are free to think or to evade that effort. But you are not free to escape from your nature, from the fact that reason is your means of survival— so that for you, who are a human being, the question 'to be or not to be' is the question 'to think or not to think.'[38]

Man lacks any instinct that would provide for his life. A lion has such a strong predation instinct that it will sometimes kill more than it can eat. Its instinct to hunt and kill is stronger than hunger. This predation instinct helps the lion to survive and thrive in this world. Man has no such instinct. Man is too small and slow to hunt. He cannot run down a rabbit, let alone a deer. Even if he could catch the deer, he lacks the physical power to overwhelm and kill it. He can outsmart his prey. He invents ways of killing the deer from a great distance. By his mind he discovers how to find water and safe foods to consume. He learns how to plant and harvest crops by using his mind. God has given man a mind to enable him to survive in this world. Therefore, a study of the heart will rightly begin with the mind.

In an earlier chapter it was shown that each person is driven by the need for unconditional love and purpose. Abraham Maslow explained that man operates on a hierarchy of needs. Before man can begin to love or care for others, his own personal needs must first be met. On every airline flight the attendants remind the passengers of the rightness of this apparently selfish tendency. On each flight, the flight attendant explains that if the cabin pressure drops everyone must put on the air mask. The passengers are told

---

[38] Ayn Rand, *Atlas Shrugged* (New York, Signet, 1957) 926

to secure their own mask before helping others. The reason is that if an individual fails to secure their own air supply, they will be useless to others. Maslow saw the basic needs of man to be food, shelter, and clothing. The Word of God sees much deeper needs than Maslow. The Bible shows that man's ultimate needs are love and purpose coming from God. Even though the Bible shows different ultimate needs than Maslow proposes, the fact that these needs must be met in each individual before they can help others is still true. A person's mind continually analyzes the current situation and strategizes to assure that these needs are met.[39]

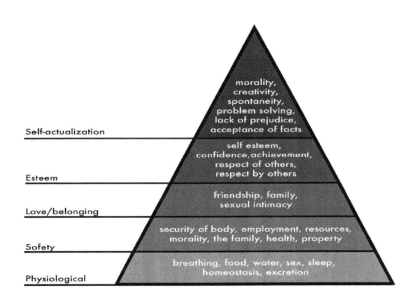

Man is designed by God to be a dependent creature. Man's first sin was an effort to live independent of God. The devil introduced to Eve the idea that something she needed could be found outside of God and His commands. He even intimated that God was a boundary preventing her from finding fulfillment[40].

[39] Image from Wikipedia, http://en.wikipedia.org/wiki/Abraham_Maslow
[40] Genesis 3:4-5 "The serpent said to the woman, 'You surely will not die! For God knows that in

When Adam and Eve believed the Devil and sought fulfillment outside of God, they brought sin to the whole human race. One of the effects of this sin is that now everyone has a bent toward seeking love and purpose outside of God. Although people know God, they suppress that truth and seek to meet their needs through creation rather than the Creator (Romans 1:18-23[41]).

The mind is where man thinks. We receive information, analyze that information, process that information in relation to other ideas we possess, and then strategize what to do with it. We may reject it as false, store it as potentially helpful, ignore it as irrelevant, or find ways to implement it for our benefit. All of this happens in the mind. Every day people are flooded with information. Some of it is so familiar that it is processed instantaneously. Someone hears a quiet beep and immediately reaches out to touch the alarm clock. They step into the kitchen and see their spouse or child and instantly respond with "Good morning!" Sometimes people face new information. They step into the kitchen and there is a stranger standing at the counter wearing a black mask. This information is shocking, and at first they do not know what to do. Quickly, their mind races to process this information. Instead of greeting the newcomer with "Good morning!" they may run away, or attack, whichever option they decide is more likely to provide for their need of safety. The mind quickly devises a strategy, and the body implements that strategy.

Every day people receive information that is false. The world is committed to personal safety and the accumulation of wealth. These are counterfeits to being loved and valued. Unless we are vigilant, we will begin to adopt the world's values. When we value safety and wealth as our ultimate needs, we find it more

---

the day you eat from it your eyes will be opened, and you will be like God, knowing good and evil.'"
[41] Romans 1:18-23 "For the wrath of God is revealed from heaven against all ungodliness and unrighteousness of men who suppress the truth in unrighteousness, because that which is known about God is evident within them; for God made it evident to them. For since the creation of the world His invisible attributes, His eternal power and divine nature, have been clearly seen, being understood through what has been made, so that they are without excuse. For even though they knew God, they did not honor Him as God or give thanks, but they became futile in their speculations, and their foolish heart was darkened. Professing to be wise, they became fools, and exchanged the glory of the incorruptible God for an image in the form of corruptible man and of birds and four-footed animals and crawling creatures."

difficult to account for God in the world. We may notice that the wicked succeed and many righteous are in grave need because God does not provide for their safety and wealth. Christians find themselves in the same dilemma as Asaph in Psalm 73. Asaph was perplexed when he saw the prosperity of the wicked. The solution for Asaph came when he entered the house of God and considered the end of the wicked (v. 17)[42] . The wicked will ultimately be destroyed. Asaph was slowly seduced by his society to believe that personal safety and wealth were signs of success. When he took the time to contemplate His God, truth began to overcome the lies. He saw that, "the nearness of God is my good," in verse 28.

Just as Asaph had to fill his mind with truth in order to resolve the apparent injustice around him, Christians today must actively fill their minds with truth. Romans 12:2 says, "Do not be conformed to this world but be transformed by the renewing of your mind..." Transformation occurs through one's thoughts. Jesus says in John 8:32, "and you will know the truth and the truth will make you free." Truth sets man free. Truth that is purposefully put into the mind frees man from failure and destruction.

The Will
Freedom is not automatic. To experience freedom each person must exercise his will. The will is the second element of the heart that needs to be considered. After people receive information, analyze it, and process it in their minds, they strategize about what they should do. This is where the will takes over. People choose the strategy that they think will be most successful, and they act in faith on that strategy. Individuals never act without their mind. For example, a person cannot accidentally stand up. One may stand up when he should have laid down or stayed seated, but standing up requires a decision. In the same way, a person cannot accidentally speak a coherent sentence. It may be possible for an accidental word to come out of the mouth, but communication requires the engagement of the mind and the determination of the will. People may speak falsely but they

---

[42] Until I came into the sanctuary of God; then I perceived their end.

cannot speak accidentally.

Take a closer look at the example of standing up to see the connection between the mind and the will. You may ask someone, "Why did you stand up in the middle of the movie?" "Because I thought it was over." The mind processed the information based on the movie. It drew the conclusion that the movie was over. The mind established a strategy to leave the theater which required standing up. The will acted. This action was an act of faith that the mind had processed the information accurately and the strategy to leave the theatre was a sound strategy. So the embarrassed movie buff stood up.

In this example, the will believed certain propositions which were in error. However, it is not the will's place to analyze, but to believe. It is vital to remember that faith resides in the will, not in the mind. James 2:26 says, "For just as the body without the spirit is dead, so also faith without works is dead." What James is pointing out is that what we really believe, we live out in our life.

If someone were to sit in your living room and tell you, "I believe that I am a chicken." You would not believe them. You would rightly conclude, "If you believe that you are a chicken, why are you seated in my living room carrying on a conversation with me? If you really believe that you are a chicken, you should act like a chicken. You should cluck and search for food with your beak, all the while avoiding people." You see, you would compare this person's words with their actions. You would base your conclusion about what they believe on their actions. You know that everyone lives what they believe.

How do you know that? Everyone believes that water comes from the faucet. People demonstrate that faith every time they place a cup under the faucet and turn the handle. Everyone believes in gravity. They demonstrate their faith by placing their spoon underneath their Cheerios. Faith resides in the will. What people believe directs their lives. What they believe is guided by their mind. No one arbitrarily chooses to act. They act in faith, believing what their mind has concluded is truth. One's mind may be wrong but his action proves his belief.

Dietrich Bonhoeffer expands this idea, "For faith is only real when there is obedience, never without it, and faith only becomes faith in the act of obedience."[43] Bonhoeffer goes to great lengths to explain and expound on the essential unity between faith and obedience. Obedience places an individual in the place where it is possible to believe. When Christ says to the rich young ruler in Matthew 19:21 "...go and sell your possessions and give to the poor, and you will have treasure in heaven; and come, follow Me." He is not giving him a new way of salvation. He is pointing out that to believe that Jesus is the living God and the only Savior, one must obey Him. He must act as though Jesus is the ruler of the universe, the source of all morality, and the right commander of mankind, if he is to believe that Jesus can forgive. The ruler's money stood in the way of such faith. Jesus brought him to a place where he could believe by demanding that he follow.

The Emotions

The third area of the heart is the emotions. Probably the greatest confusion about the heart revolves around the emotions. For many, emotions are like sensors that discover hidden dangers in the situations around them. Others refer to being led by their emotions, believing that somehow their emotions affect the way that they think. Both of these concepts are inconsistent with the

Biblical teaching about emotions. Emotions are not an active element of our heart that can sense problems, discover danger, or drive one's thinking. Often people pay closer attention to their emotions than to what drives their emotions so that it appears, at first glance, that their emotions are leading them. However, such focus does not change the reality that emotions are **always** a passive response to one's thinking and the success of one's volitional choices.

Imagine placing a rattlesnake next to an infant. Will the newborn experience the emotion of fear? Of course not! Why not? Because the child does not "know" that the snake is dangerous. Everyone recognizes immediately that the mind produces the emotion of fear regarding the rattlesnake. The

---

[43] Dietrich Bonhoeffer, (2012-08-07). *The Cost of Discipleship* .64 Kindle Edition.

emotion is a response to the thinking. Imagine that the infant has grown up. The infant is now a herpetologist who specializes in rattlesnakes. Will he be afraid? He will be cautious, but his years of experience with snakes will help him to anticipate the snake's behavior and avoid a painful strike. He will carefully move away, fully aware that if he moves slowly, the snake will not sense danger and will not strike.

On the other hand, if you put the snake next to some untrained adults, they will be filled with terror. They are convinced that all snakes are malicious creatures that exist to sneak up on people and kill them with either their venomous bite or their creepy touch. Such wrong thinking leads to fear. A snake-loving friend might assist them to overcome their fear of snakes by instructing them about snakes. They would explain which snakes are venomous and the fact that even venomous snakes do not want to waste their venom on people since people are too big to eat. To the extent that someone learns from the snake lover (thus engaging the mind with truth) and believes it to be true, putting it into practice (the will), they are freed from the emotion of fear.

Summary
The greatest commandment is found in Deuteronomy 6:5, "You shall love the Lord your God with all your heart, and with all your soul and with all your might." The heart includes the mind, will, and emotions. With the mind people process information and develop strategies to meet their deepest needs to be loved and valued. With the will one implements these strategies. The emotions respond to the success in meeting the needs identified by the mind. When we remember that God is all that we need, and then choose to rest in Him by demonstrating love to those around us, we find real peace and joy. And that is a good thing!

4 THE TRAIN

And do not be conformed to this world, but be transformed by the renewing of your mind, that you may prove what the will of God is, that which is good and acceptable and perfect.
Romans 12:2

"Annette, I know I have been a jerk lately. Thank you for telling me how you feel. I am sorry that I have been so caught up in everything else in life that I have neglected you. I now know that I have been selfish, only thinking of myself. I will change. Annette, I want you to know that I love you."

The silence that followed lasted only a few seconds, but Carl felt it was an hour. Annette just looked at him, wondering if he meant what he had said. They were the right words. He understood her concern, but was he saying these things because he was truly broken? Maybe he just wanted to get her back.

Carl and Annette had been married for ten years. Shortly after their wedding, Carl became more focused on himself. He quit going to the movies that Annette liked. He played cards with the guys every Monday, and their dates became more and more rare. Their sexual relationship had been exciting at first. They had "played around" while they dated, so it was freeing to make love without guilt. As time passed, Annette sensed a change. Carl was less interested in her pleasure. In fact she began to feel that she was just a tool for him to make himself feel better. Whenever she thought about that, she would cry. Last week, Annette took *their sons; and moved into her parent's house. She told Carl that things had to change.*

After his meeting with Annette, Carl's day was horrible. He remembered the awkward silence after he told Annette that he loved her. The question, "Why didn't she tell me she loved me?" kept pulsing through his mind. He thought about the ways he had cared for her. Her made a good income and allowed Annette to buy the things she wanted. He was kind. He rarely yelled at her. He was active at church, so he was obviously caring for her spiritual needs. Why couldn't she just tell him that she loved him too? The thought haunted him. He was a little angry at Annette for her failure. He was also afraid that if she could not say "I love you." they might end up divorced. Throughout the day, both of these emotions grew.

In order to become proficient in any activity, one of the most important questions we can ask is, "Why?" Most people have painted a wall at some point in their lives. Anyone can put paint on a wall. However, an accomplished painter has answered the question "why?" He knows why he should wash the wall, prime the bare wood and sand the previous finish. When a person understands why he is taking a particular action, he can apply that same principle to other situations. One needs to prime the bare wood to increase adhesion of the top coat and to assist the top coat with an even absorption, providing an even finish. Knowing this, he can deduce that he does not need to prime a previously painted wall. The earlier finish will accomplish what the primer was intended to provide. He also understands that if a primer is designed to help the top coat stick to it, then he needs to put a top coat on it, or it will allow dirt to adhere to it as well. Knowing "why?" helps a person expand his ability to succeed in his painting projects.

The last chapter explained the parts of the heart: the mind, the will and the emotions. The mind processes information and develops strategies to meet one's needs. The will acts in faith by implementing these strategies. The emotions respond to the success, or failure of these strategies. By seeing what each part does, people have a better ability to bring emotional health to their lives. However, guarding their hearts (Proverbs 4:23[44]) requires them to also understand how the parts work together.

The elements of the heart work together just like the cars on a train. The emotions are like the caboose. They follow the will, responding to the success, or failure of the choices the will has made. The will is the freight car. It carries the important cargo, namely faith, and it is pulled down the tracks by the mind. The mind is the engine of *The Train*. It alone possesses motive power: the ability to initiate and move the heart. It is essential to note that this is **NOT** how the heart **should** work. This is how it **does** work; always. The emotions cannot lead the heart, ever. Just as a caboose cannot pull a train because it has no engine, the emotions cannot initiate thinking or choices. The emotions always respond. In the same way, the will cannot act without some purpose. This is the flaw of the existentialist idea that faith is a blind leap into the unknown. No one actually fully leaps into the unknown apart from the mind. Such a leap requires the mind to weigh the options and the will to believe that the "unknown" is preferable, or at least potentially preferable, to the known. Upon drawing this conclusion, the will acts by leaping. Faith must have some cognitive motivator. It is always led by the mind.

Consider the diagram below.

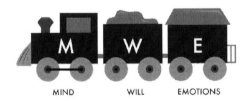

MIND   WILL   EMOTIONS

Transformed Mind

Various passages of Scripture demonstrate that faith is led by the mind. In Romans 12:2 Paul writes, "And do not be conformed to this world, but be transformed by the renewing of

---

[44] Proverbs 4:23 "Watch over your heart with all diligence, for from it flow the springs of life."

your mind, that you may prove what the will of God is, that which is good and acceptable and perfect." Transformation of the Christian's life occurs not through a simple appeal to the will. Instead, God appeals to the mind to be renewed. The will follows the mind. That is why in 2 Corinthians 10:5 Paul writes, "We are destroying speculations and every lofty thing raised up against the knowledge of God, and we are taking every thought captive to the obedience of Christ…" Notice that taking thoughts captive, that is to fill one's mind only with truth, leads to obedience: actions of the will in conformity with the will of God.

The word that the NASB has translated as "world" in Romans 12:2 is *"αιόν."* *"Αιόν"* is best translated as "age." Herman Sasse explains the use of *αιόν*: "The term is used in philosophical discussions of time, usually for a span of time as distinct from time as such (*χρονόσ*)."[45] So Romans commands people to not be conformed to their current age. The most common word for "world" is *"κοσμόσ."* Paul frequently sets the *kosmos* against God and His Church. He speaks of the wisdom of the world as being foolishness to God (1 Corinthians 1:20).[46] Jesus, in His High Priestly prayer, repeatedly mentions that His disciples are not "of the world."[47] They are distinct from the world system that is in opposition to God and His Church.

The word *αιόν*, when translated as "world," ordinarily speaks in a more generic sense of the world and often can refer to that which includes both the wicked and the righteous. In the great parable of the wheat and the tares,[48] the field is said to be the world, *αιόν*. It is the physical planet on which people live that Jesus had in view. The choice of the word *αιόν* in Romans 12 expands the command against conformity. Paul did not say to merely avoid being like non-Christians. He tells God's people that they should never conform to anything on the earth. Conformity

---

[45], Gerhard Friedrich Kittel, *Theological Dictionary of the New Testament, abridged edition*, (Grand Rapids, William B. Eerdmans Publishing Company Biblesoft Inc1985).
[46] 1 Corinthians 1:20 "Where is the wise man? Where is the scribe? Where is the debater of this age? Has not God made foolish the wisdom of the world?"
[47] John 17:16 "They are not of the world, even as I am not of the world."
[48] Matthew 13:38, "and the field is the world; and as for the good seed, these are the sons of the kingdom; and the tares are the sons of the evil one."

involves allowing external pressure to form someone. Instead, God desires transformation; the purposeful choice to follow God and His commands. This transformation occurs as people's minds are renewed, when they are continually filled with truth. Transformation begins in the intellectual faculty of the heart. Surely it is not completed in the mind but must include the whole heart. Paul understood that the heart is **always** directed by truth processed through the mind.

Believe Truth

Truth in the mind is the first step. Since people's minds are deeply concerned with their greatest needs, to be loved and valued, the truth that should be central in their mind is that God is all that they need. People must be convinced through Scripture and regular meditation that God loves them unconditionally and that He has created them with a unique purpose in this world: a purpose which reflects God's glory as no one else is able to do. This truth, that God meets all of their needs, enables them to develop right strategies which they implement through their will. However, people do not always believe the truth.

For a healthy life, one must not only know the truth, he must also believe truth. Faith is an act of the will. James 2:26 says, "For just as the body without the spirit is dead, so also faith without works is dead." Earlier in his epistle, James compared professing one's faith and living one's faith. He is showing that faith is not exclusively an intellectual activity. Faith is a volitional action, based on intellectual information. Francis Schaeffer spoke of "sufficient evidence" upon which to place one's faith. Schaeffer recognized that there exists a distinction between intellectual assent and faith.

As people develop strategies for meeting their needs, they act in faith on those strategies. If they believe that God is all that they need, their strategy is simple: they are free to risk rejection and failure to love the people around them. They do not need anyone to love or value them, so they do not need to be guarded as they reach out to others with the love of Jesus. They are free to freely forgive those who offend them. They are free to confess their failures because Jesus has forgiven them (Romans 8:31-33[49]). Righteous actions are possible as they believe the simple truth that God is all that they need.

However, sometimes people choose to pursue the love and value that men can provide. A man may reject the truth that God is all that he needs and believe instead that he needs his wife to respect him. It is not wrong to want his wife to respect him. It is wrong to look to her to meet his need of being valued.

Broken Cisterns

This subtle distinction is what led to God's indictment of the nation of Judah in Jeremiah 2:13. "For My people have committed two evils: they have forsaken Me, the fountain of living waters, to hew for themselves cisterns, broken cisterns, that can hold no water." A cistern is not a well. It is used to catch and contain rain water primarily to water the livestock. At its very best a cistern provides stagnant, impure water. When the cistern is broken, the livestock enter it and stand in the water, further fouling the water with their feet and by urinating and defecating in the water. This is the image that God gives of man's efforts to have their needs met by people. When we seek our needs to be met by anyone or anything other than God, we have chosen to drink from the polluted water of a broken cistern. Although, like in a cistern, there may be some remnants of love and value, these are polluted by the inconsistency and imperfection of sinful man.

BROKEN CISTERN

---

[49] Romans 8:31-33 "What then shall we say to these things? If God is for us, who is against us? 32 He who did not spare His own Son, but delivered Him over for us all, how will He not also with Him freely give us all things? 33 Who will bring a charge against God's elect? God is the one who justifies..."

Instead of seeking all of our needs in God, we frequently forsake Him who can satisfy our souls in order to quench our thirst in polluted water. When we do, we place certain expectations on the people around us. We expect these people to affirm our value and to love us. We place these expectations on others because, at that moment, we believe that we need the love and value that people can provide. When these expectations are met, it feels pleasant. If they are not met, it feels bad.

Negative Emotions

The purpose of negative emotions is to indicate that someone is thinking and believing a lie. Just like a warning light on a car, emotions communicate the need to take action quickly. One day a man started his car and saw the "check engine" light shining brightly on the dashboard. He had never encountered this before, so he shut off the car and found another means of transportation. He did not know what the problem was, but it must be important because a light came on to tell him to check his engine. In the same way, God gives us certain emotions to communicate the need to check our thinking, and faith commitments.

Consider three emotions: anger, fear, and guilt. Chapter one demonstrated that anger does not belong in the Christian's life. In 1 John 4:18 God says, "There is no fear in love; but perfect love casts out fear, because fear involves punishment, and the one who fears is not perfected in love." If someone fears, they are not perfected in love. Jesus even says, in Matthew 10:28[50], to not be afraid of someone who is able to kill the body. Fear is not appropriate in a Christian's life. In Romans 8:1 Paul writes, "There is therefore now no condemnation for those who are in Christ Jesus." No condemnation—then why would we have a sense of guilt? Guilt, which is a sense of worthlessness, does not belong in the Christian life. Each of these emotions is a response to the strategies to meet one's needs outside of God. Each is the result of wrong expectations that are placed upon the people and situations in one's life.

---

[50] Matthew 10:28 ""Do not fear those who kill the body but are unable to kill the soul; but rather fear Him who is able to destroy both soul and body in hell."

57

Anger is the result of a *blocked expectation*. When you place an expectation on a person or a situation in order to fulfill your need to be loved or valued and that expectation is not realized, you respond with anger. When you are *uncertain* of the possibility of meeting your needs through your *expectation*, you experience fear. Compare this idea with 1 John 4:18, "There is no fear in love; but perfect love casts out fear, because fear involves punishment, and the one who fears is not perfected in love." The one who fears has not been perfected in love. If one loves perfectly, he places no expectations on the people around him. Instead he lays down his life in order to express the love of God to them. When someone is not sure if people will love or value them; that is they are unsure if others will meet their expectations and subsequently their needs, they experience fear. When one's *expectation* is simply *unreachable,* one feels guilty. An example of this is when someone believes that he must not fail the people around him.

A common expectation experienced by Christian parents is that they expect their child to know the love of God. They try loving discipline, regular devotions, church attendance, and gracious patience with their child's failures, but still some children turn away from Jesus. The parents are racked with a deep sense of failure because their expectation, that the child should embrace the gospel, is not something the parents can ever accomplish. All they can do is love the child. The child's choice to know the love of God is beyond the parent's control and therefore is a wrong expectation for the parent.

Consider a parent living with the expectation that their child must follow Jesus. Imagine the anxiety that the parent feels when their child is in a tempting situation. Consider the frustration when the child chooses to rebel. How overwhelming is the guilt when the child turns away? The parents will ask, "What did we do wrong?" Do you see the *uncertain expectation,* the *blocked expectation,* and the *unreachable expectation?*

Desires or Expectations
Expectations grow out of strong desires for good things. It

is good for people to be loved and valued by those nearest them. It is good for one's children to believe. It is good for the driver of the other car to be careful when passing your car. Most people desire these things. Somewhere along the path, our desires get confused, and w begin to think and believe that we need these good things. We forget the simple truth that Jesus is all that we need, so we adopt another strategy for meeting our needs. We seek our love and value from the people around us (those lovely broken cisterns) and we place expectations on others to meet our needs. We then begin the work of manipulating our loved ones in order to get what we wrongly believe we need.

Simply put, it is wrong for someone to place expectations on anyone other than himself. As soon as he places an expectation on someone or something other than himself, he has given up control of his emotions. Now the other person can *make* him happy or angry. Their actions, and not his, are the key to his emotional stability. Galatians 5:1 says, "It was for freedom that Christ set us free; therefore, keep standing firm and do not be subject again to a yoke of slavery." A man's expectations placed on his wife enslaves that man. They also become a tool for him to try to enslave her.

A definition of proper desires and proper expectations might be useful. A proper desire is "any legitimate want over which one **does not** have total control." A woman may want the car to start, her friends to respect her or her children to obey. All of these are good desires but none of them is under her control. A proper expectation is any legitimate want over which one **does** have total control. The only thing in this world that a person fully controls is himself. Proper expectations are expectations over your own thoughts and actions. The one certain proper expectation is to love. If you can choose, in every interaction with people, to love them, your emotions will testify to the rightness of this choice by peace and joy filling your life.

How do you know when your desire for something good has become an expectation? That is why God gave you *anger, fear, and guilt.* These three emotions communicate to you that you have forgotten that God is all that you need, and you believe that something other than Him is necessary for your needs to be met. We need to learn how to hear, and trust these emotions.

Summary

It is important to know, not just what the parts of the heart are, but how they work together. The heart works like a train. The mind provides the energy for action. People act upon what they think. The will is driven by the mind. In it people exercise faith by developing desires and expectations. When their thinking is right, they choose to place expectations only on themselves. Emotions respond to our success at fulfilling our expectations. When the expectations are improper, we often face anger, fear and guilt. Anger is the result of a *blocked expectation*. Fear results from an *uncertain expectation*. Guilt comes from an *unreachable expectation*. This is the only way the heart can work. By recognizing and believing this truth, we will have a tool that helps us change our wrong thinking and experience the joy and peace which Jesus provides.

The next morning, Carl met with Earl for breakfast. Earl was a good friend from Church. They had known each other for a couple of years. People at church respected Earl, and Carl liked to meet with him. They met every other week. After Carl explained what had happened yesterday with Annette, Earl asked, "Why does it upset you that Annette did not tell you she loves you?"

"Isn't it obvious? Shouldn't a man be upset when his wife doesn't love him?"

"Not necessarily. Does the Bible ever command you to be loved by your wife? Can you control whether she loves you or not? Does her love, or lack of love, actually prevent you from finding true happiness or fulfillment in life?"

"I never thought of it that way. I just thought that a woman ought to love her husband."

"She should. However, that is between her and God. Her

love neither adds to, nor detracts from, what the husband actually needs."

Earl continued, "Does the Bible command you to love your wife?"

"Have you consistently loved Annette?"

"No. I guess I haven't. In fact, I have been pretty focused on me for most of our marriage."

Earl paused for just a moment to allow the ideas to sink into Carl's mind. "So you are more upset that she doesn't show you love than you are at you own failure to love her."

"Oh, my goodness! When I am upset that she didn't say she loves me, I am just thinking about me again. Will I ever learn?"

"I think you are learning. Repentance requires that you know how you have sinned. That is why God let you feel rotten yesterday. Your emotions were a reminder to you that you were looking to Annette to meet your needs. You forgot that God is all you need. You expected God plus Annette to love you. Carl, trust that Jesus loves you and you will be free to show Annette the love He has for her."

"Earl, I really appreciate you. Will you pray for us?"

Pulling out his billfold, Carl said, "Breakfast is on me this week."

VINCENT L. WOOD

5 FEAR AND GUILT

By this, love is perfected with us, that we may have confidence in the day of judgment; because as He is, so also are we in this world. There is no fear in love; but perfect love casts out fear, because fear involves punishment, and the one who fears is not perfected in love.
1 John 4:17-18

In the hit series *Monk*, the main character, Adrian Monk, is paralyzed by his fears. In fact, he has more than 100 phobias ranging from tight places to germs. In one episode, Adrian and his assistant Sharona are trying to solve a murder involving a circus. When they speak to an elephant trainer, Sharona confesses her fear of elephants. Adrian laughs and tells her to just "suck it up." This man, who uses a wipe after shaking hands for fear of germs, ridicules a woman for being afraid of elephants.[51] This funny scene hits close to home. Most people believe that their own fears are rational while the fears other people have are silly.

Comedian Jerry Seinfeld observed that the number one fear in America is public speaking, while number two is death. Seinfeld points out that this means that at a funeral most people would rather be in the casket than giving the eulogy.[52] Many

---

[51] *Monk, "Mr. Monk Goes to the Circus," Episode no.17.* first broadcast 18 July, 2003 by US Cable Entertainment, Directed by Randal Zisk and written by James Krieg.
[52] *Seinfeld, "The Pilot (1)," Episode no. 62.* First broadcast 20 May, 1993 by NBC. Directed by Tom Cherones and written by Jerry Seinfeld.

people assume that fear is based on actual danger. People think that when they are afraid it is because their emotions sense a potentially dangerous situation and respond by sending adrenaline to their body to prepare them to act when the danger poses the greatest threat. Fear is like a sensor that scans the situation around a person and warns of any potential problems. With this view, people have a hard time understanding passages of Scripture that tell them to not be afraid. Fear is actually an emotional response based on one's thinking about a particular situation. For example, a newborn baby placed next to a rattlesnake does not feel any fear because it does not know that the snake poses a danger. One's emotions always follow one's thinking.

The last chapter discussed expectations. People establish expectations in a given situation based on what they believe they need to occur. They convince themselves that they need someone to demonstrate love to them or to affirm their value. They become afraid when there is a reasonable possibility that their expectation will not be met. Fear alerts them to an uncertain expectation which is based on wrong thinking.

Forty-seven times the NASB uses the exact clause, "do not be afraid." Just to understand how often that is, the NASB only uses the clause, "praise the Lord" forty-three times. Every Christian would acknowledge how important it is to praise the Lord, but we rarely think about how important it is to not fear. God told Joshua in Joshua 1:9, "Have I not commanded you? Be strong and courageous! Do not tremble or be dismayed, for the Lord your God is with you wherever you go." Joshua is to believe that God is with him instead of being afraid of the enemies in Canaan. Fear is in direct opposition to faith, and "without faith it is impossible to please God."[53]

Look at 1 John 4:18, "There is no fear in love; but perfect love casts out fear, because fear involves punishment, and the one who fears is not perfected in love." John did not write that love allows a little fear or that fear in some dangerous situations is reasonable. He said that love casts out fear. If one is afraid, that person is not

---

[53] Hebrews 11:6

perfected (or completed) in love. This directly opposes our common understanding of fear. Jesus says in Matthew 10:28, "And do not fear those who kill the body, but are unable to kill the soul; but rather fear Him who is able to destroy both soul and body in hell." Jesus says that a believer does not need to be afraid of dying. Even if someone who hates you holds a gun to your head, you can be free from fear. How can you gain such courage?

Freedom from fear begins with your mind. You must know the truth. The truth is that you do not need to continue to live in this body. You may want to continue to live in your body, but you do not need to. God is able to sustain your life or He can take it at any time that pleases Him. Your life is truly in His hands, and He loves you more than you can imagine. Jesus combined these two ideas when He was speaking with Pilate the day He died. In John 19:10-11 John writes,

> Pilate therefore said to Him, 'You do not speak to me? Do You not know that I have authority to release You, and I have authority to crucify You?' Jesus answered, 'You would have no authority over Me, unless it had been given you from above; for this reason he who delivered Me up to you has the greater sin.'

When Pilate threatens Jesus' life, Jesus does not cower in fear. He instead speaks truth to Pilate. Jesus affirms His faith that the Father is in control. In acknowledging this fact, Jesus also remembers that His Father adores Him. If the one who controls the universe loves you personally, what do you need to fear? Paul puts it this way in Romans 8:31, "If God is for us, who can be against us?"

Paul, who was facing the possibility of execution when He wrote to the Church in Philippi, expresses this same idea. He writes in Philippians 1:21, "for to me to live is Christ and to die is gain." He did not fear death because he knew that death was a servant who would open the throne room door for him to enter into the presence of his loving Savior. Paul knew of no greater treasure than to be near Jesus. The executioner would only speed this along. He was ready.

As a believer, you do not need to fear death, but what about difficulties, persecutions, or pain? We might say something like, "I am not afraid of death. I'm afraid of dying." Consider James 1:2-3, "Consider it all joy, my brethren, when you encounter various trials, knowing that the testing of your faith produces endurance." Trials produce something valuable in your life; endurance. Endurance is valuable because inherent in endurance is faith. Romans 5:3-5 says,

> And not only this, but we also exult in our tribulations, knowing that tribulation brings about perseverance; and perseverance, proven character; and proven character, hope; and hope does not disappoint, because the love of God has been poured out within our hearts through the Holy Spirit who was given to us.

Hardship ultimately produces hope. Hardship points you to something better than life in a sin-cursed world. People just have a hard time *believing* that life outside of this sin-cursed world is better.

Fear does not belong in the Christian's life. It is removed by filling the mind with truth and choosing to act in faith upon that truth. In Daniel 3:15-18, King Nebuchadnezzar confronts the three Hebrew children who would not worship his idol: "…But if you will not worship, you will immediately be cast into the midst of a furnace of blazing fire; and what god is there who can deliver you out of my hands?" Nebuchadnezzar wanted the Hebrew children to believe that death would end their lives. They refused and instead believed, saying,

> O Nebuchadnezzar, we do not need to give you an answer concerning this matter. If it be so, our God whom we serve is able to deliver us from the furnace of blazing fire; and He will deliver us out of

> your hand, O king. But even if He does not, let it be
> known to you, O king, that we are not going to
> serve your gods or worship the golden image that
> you have set up.

They knew that after their death, they would live with God forever.

People are inundated with temptations to believe that this life is all there is. The world system in which they live is based on this idea, and it opposes those who try to live like eternal beings. Sadly, even in the Church, people can lose sight of the truth of eternity. One of the great benefits of personal worship each morning is that the believer is reminded that he belongs to God and can find freedom to rise above the realm of fear. When you rise early to pray and read Scripture, you are exercising faith. You are bringing your whole heart to God because you believe that He is, and that He loves you. "And without faith it is impossible to please Him, for he who comes to God must believe that He is and that He is a rewarder of those who seek Him" (Hebrews 11:6). Notice the first act of faith is to come to God, to pursue Him. It is essential to seek God daily, to set aside the time to listen to Him in His Word. Listen to the love He has for you. Meditate on that love and the acceptance you have in the presence of the only true God. When you have filled your mind with this reality, pray. Talk to the God who adores you. Share your joys and your sadness with Him, confident of His concern. Ask Him for help as you think about the coming day.

Guilt

Too many people in the Church live their lives with a sense of unworthiness, or worse yet, worthlessness. They feel that they are a disappointment to God and to the people around them. These people are keenly aware of their own failures. This sense of guilt leaves them depressed, fearful, and unmotivated. When a Christian is overwhelmed with the feeling of being unacceptable, he has forgotten the basic premise of the gospel and is prevented from reaching out to other people. He is trapped. God's intention for guilt as a sense of actual moral failure is for it to lead to confession and repentance. Consider 2 Corinthians 7:10-11:

> For the sorrow that is according to the will of God produces a repentance without regret, leading to salvation; but the sorrow of the world produces death. For behold what earnestness this very thing, this godly sorrow, has produced in you: what vindication of yourselves, what indignation, what fear, what longing, what zeal, what avenging of wrong! In everything you demonstrated yourselves to be innocent in the matter.

In this chapter, the word "guilt" refers to a debilitating sense of worthlessness. In John Bunyan's classic work, *The Pilgrim's Progress*, he describes this sense of guilt that can overwhelm a Christian. The main character, Christian, weary from his travels and assuming a side path will save some time, wanders off the straight and narrow way that leads to the Celestial City. Soon the weather turns bad, and he is captured by the giant, Despair, who takes him to Doubting Castle. The giant throws Christian into the Dungeon of Despair where he tortures him. One night Christian comes to his senses and realizes that he has a key in his pocket that will open any lock in Doubting Castle. That key is called the Promises of God. With this key, Christian is soon free and walking on the right path again.

Jesus said that He came to set the captives free.[54] He does not mean that He wants to empty the jails of criminals. Guilt is one of the oppressors whom Jesus destroys for a Christian.[55] In Galatians 5:1, Paul said to oppressed Christians, "It was for freedom that Christ set us free; therefore keep standing firm and do not be subject again to a yoke of slavery." This is an important work even today: to set free those who are captured by guilt, empowering them to stand firm.

---

[54] Luke 4:18 "The Spirit of the LORD is upon me, because He has anointed me to preach the gospel to the poor. He has sent me to proclaim release to the captives, and recovery of sight to the blind, to set free those who are oppressed,"

[55] Romans 8:1 "Therefore there is now no condemnation for those who are in Christ Jesus."

The power to stand firm comes from the gospel. 1 Corinthians 15:3-4 explains what this gospel is, "For I delivered to you as of first importance what I also received, that Christ died for our sins according to the Scriptures, and that He was buried, and that He was raised on the third day according to the Scriptures…" The gospel declares that Jesus bore all of the punishment due for all of the sins of His people. This idea demands more than lip-service. If Jesus bore the entire wrath of God for your sins, then God has no wrath for you, not even a little. Instead, He forgives you based on Jesus' substitutionary sacrifice. Because God's wrath is fully satisfied in Jesus, when you fail, God is free to express love and mercy to you. This love and mercy empowers you to repent (Romans 2:4).[56]

In addition to forgiving your sins, God declared you righteous. Your righteousness is not something that you earned by obeying the law. It is what Jesus earned by obeying the law. Just as the guilt for your sin was placed on Jesus, the "guilt" for His righteousness was placed on you. You receive the full benefit of His obedience, which is complete reconciliation with God. God, who said, "Let there be light," and "there was light," said of each believer, "He is righteous."

Consider how the book of Proverbs uses the idea of "righteous." The word "righteous" is used sixty-six times. Each time, the word is used in contrast with the wicked, or fools. Which one do you immediately relate to? Most people associate with the righteous. The righteous are those who put their trust in God. They are believers like Abraham. "Abraham believed God and He reckoned it to him as righteousness." Consider the following passages. Genesis 15:6 "Then he believed in the Lord; and He reckoned it to him as righteousness." Romans 4:3 "For what does the Scripture say? 'Abraham believed God, and it was credited to him as righteousness.'" Galatians 3:6 "Even so Abraham believed God, and it was reckoned to him as righteousness." James 2:23 "and the Scripture was fulfilled which says, 'And Abraham believed God, and it was reckoned to him as righteousness,' and he

---

[56] Romans 2:4 "Or do you think lightly of the riches of His kindness and tolerance and patience, not knowing that the kindness of God leads you to repentance?"

was called the friend of God. "

It is not their obedience that makes believers righteous. Instead the imputed righteousness of Jesus enables believers to obey. The imputed righteousness of Christ is the wellspring from which their sanctification rises. This is why, throughout Scripture, God refers to His Church, not as a collection of sinners, but as saints. In Psalm 16:3, David writes, "As for the saints who are in the earth, they are the majestic ones in whom is all my delight." The saints are the chosen people of God. They are the holy ones, His spotless bride. God has set them apart for Himself. He forgives all of their sins and authoritatively declares them righteous.

The fact that God declares believers righteous is a freeing truth. Christians can begin to see themselves and each other as God sees them. Such a perspective enables each person to live up to that reality. This pattern is evidenced in the book of Ephesians. In chapters 1-3, Paul explains all that God has done for Christians. In chapter two, He says that Christians "were dead in our trespasses and sins" in which they used to walk. Notice the past tense. The saints at Ephesus do not walk that way any longer. They are no longer dead. Now they are very much alive in Christ because of the great love of God. Even though their past, including yesterday, is filled with personal failure, they are accepted fully by God because Jesus paid their debt and gave them His righteousness. This is the gospel that sets people free.

In chapter 4:1, Paul uses the word "therefore" before exhorting the church to "walk in a manner worthy of the calling…" W. Foerester points out, in *The Theological Dictionary of the New Testament*, that the word translated "worthy," *axios,* "Strictly" means "bringing into balance." The balance is found as the work of justification empowers the believer for a life of righteousness. Since the believer is forgiven, declared righteous, adopted and empowered by God's Spirit, he can now "…lay aside the old self, which is being corrupted in accordance with the lusts of deceit, and that he be renewed in the spirit of his mind (Ephesians 4:22-23). This real life transformation is the outworking of the Christian's justification. Having found reconciliation with God, the believer is free to live consistent with, or worthy of, that salvation.

Another crucial idea that sets the prisoner free is the reality of his freedom in Christ. The believer is free from sin. In Romans chapter 6 Paul explains this truth. Paul begins the chapter with a question, "Are we to continue in sin that grace might increase?" His short answer is "May it never be!" Those who are in Christ have died to sin. Why would they want to live in sin any longer?

Paul uses the words, μή γενοίτα which we translate "may it never be." Do not miss the force of this statement by Paul. The word μή means "not" and it precedes the word it modifies. Γενοίτα is the basis of our word "generate." It means "to bring into existence." It is used three times in John 1:3, "All things came into being by Him, and apart from Him nothing came into being that has come into being." The NASB translates it "come into being" while showing that the active element of all existence is Jesus, the Word of God. This same word is the one Paul chooses to express, in the strongest terms possible, the absurdity of continuing in sin to gain more grace. He uses it again in Romans 6:15.[57] The English translation carries a subjunctive tone, as if it isn't likely. In the Greek, there is no uncertainty. Paul, in essence, says, "It cannot even exist."

When you die to life, life no longer has any power over you. Paul says, in Ephesians 2:1,[58] that non-Christians are dead *in* sin. They are incapable of living actions and unable to respond to any external stimuli. Here in Romans 6 he declares that believers are dead *to* sin. Sin has no power in their lives. That is not to say that they no longer sin. Paul's point is that once the power of sin has been broken in your life, why would you want to live in it any longer? It is as absurd as the man who wants to spend his life in a coffin.

Paul presupposes that sin is bad. That is to say, that it is not just inconsistent with God's law, but it is in fact, ontologically,

---

[57] Romans 6:15 "What then? Shall we sin because we are not under law but under grace? May it never be!"
[58] Ephesians 2:1 "And you were dead in your trespasses and sins,"

bad. Sin is in opposition to that which is good. That which is bad is always bad for you. So once the power of the bad has been removed, why continue in it? You now have power to do good (Ephesians 2:10[59]).

Next, Paul asks the question in verse 15, "Shall we sin because we are not under law but under grace?" Once again the answer is "May it never be." Here Paul begins to address the idea of the right to command. Paul answers this question by discussing the fact that Christians are no longer slaves to sin. An owner has the right to command his own slaves. Since Christians are no longer owned by sin—they were bought with a price (1 Corinthians 6:20[60])—they do not need to obey their former owner, sin. When sin says to the believer, "You must respond in anger, fear, or guilt," the Christian is free to say, "Go jump in a lake. I do not have to listen to you. My new master commands me to love my enemy, and that is what I will do!"

Sadly, many have switched the messages. To those who do not know Jesus, that is, those who are living in rebellion against God, they communicate, "God loves you and has a wonderful plan for your life." There is no question about the importance of presenting the love of God to lost sinners,[61] and yet that seems to be the message reserved for God's people (Jeremiah 29:11-13).[62] The message given to the Church, whom God adores and whom He calls "My beloved," is "God is angry with your sin. Repent, you brood of vipers." Christians read the sermon preached by Jonathon Edwards, *Sinners in the Hands of an Angry God* without recognizing that Edwards preached that message to the unconverted in his congregation in order to bring a great revival. The target audience was not for the people of God but for the unredeemed living among God's people. The messages get

---

[59] Ephesians 2:10 "For we are His workmanship, created in Christ Jesus for good works, which God prepared beforehand so that we would walk in them."

[60] 1 Corinthians 6:20 "For you have been bought with a price: therefore glorify God in your body."

[61] John 3:16 "For God so loved the world, that He gave His only begotten Son, that whoever believes in Him shall not perish, but have eternal life."

[62] Jeremiah 29:11-13 "'For I know the plans that I have for you,' declares the Lord, 'plans for welfare and not for calamity to give you a future and a hope. 12 'Then you will call upon Me and come and pray to Me, and I will listen to you. 13 'You will seek Me and find Me when you search for Me with all your heart."

confused. God's beloved are told that He is angry with them. This message alienates them from the One who adores them. The rebellious, who reject Jesus, are convinced that God is okay with them. Sadly, the unbelievers believe this message, seeing no need to change.

Imagine if the Church got the message right. To the unsaved, she expresses the great danger that they face. She explains that God's wrath, which they will rightly face, is a consuming fire that never relents. Such a message may encourage them to flee the wrath to come. Such a message may help them recognize that their life justly deserves God's wrath and displeasure. It might lead them to turn to Christ for mercy. And if the Church helped the people of God comprehend the richness of God's love (Ephesians 3:14-19),[63] they might begin to understand the real power they possess to overcome every temptation they face (1 Corinthians 10:13 and Romans 6). In Christian ministry, that is precisely the goal. We seek to convince the people of God of the reality of their position before God. As Christians understand this truth, we encourage them to believe it, acting in their faith (James 2:17-22)[64] and finding freedom from sin, so that they may actually practice righteous deeds (Ephesians 2:10).

Summary
Believers around the world are tormented by fear and guilt. God tells His people that they need not fear and that their guilt is removed. Much of the anguish that people face is due to forgetting these simple truths. As Christians, we need to remind people of the reality of the gospel: Jesus loves and values His people and He has set them free. With this gospel, we can join in Jesus' work of

---

[63] Ephesians 3:14-19 "For this reason I bow my knees before the Father, from whom every family in heaven and on earth derives its name, that He would grant you, according to the riches of His glory, to be strengthened with power through His Spirit in the inner man, so that Christ may dwell in your hearts through faith; and that you, being rooted and grounded in love, may be able to comprehend with all the saints what is the breadth and length and height and depth, and to know the love of Christ which surpasses knowledge, that you may be filled up to all the fullness of God."

[64] James 2:17-22" Even so faith, if it has no works, is dead, being by itself. But someone may well say, "You have faith and I have works; show me your faith without the works, and I will show you my faith by my works." You believe that God is one. You do well; the demons also believe, and shudder. But are you willing to recognize, you foolish fellow, that faith without works is useless? Was not Abraham our father justified by works when he offered up Isaac his son on the altar? You see that faith was working with his works, and as a result of the works, faith was perfected..."

setting captives free.

6 PHILIPPIANS 4:6-9

*Be anxious for nothing, but in everything by prayer
and supplication with thanksgiving let your requests
be made known to God. And the peace of God,
which surpasses all comprehension, shall guard
your hearts and your minds in Christ Jesus.*

*Finally, brethren, whatever is true, whatever is
honorable, whatever is right, whatever is pure,
whatever is lovely, whatever is of good repute, if
there is any excellence and if anything worthy of
praise, let your mind dwell on these things. The
things you have learned and received and heard
and seen in me, practice these things; and the God
of peace shall be with you.*

The heart works like a train. The mind is the engine which informs and directs the will. The emotions, functioning like a caboose, respond to the will. If you successfully meet the will's expectation, you usually feel good. If you fail, you feel bad. This understanding of the heart acknowledges that each person is responsible for and able to control their own emotions. People are set free from the tyranny of having to feel a certain way. The apostle Paul commends this idea in Romans 12:2[65] as he

---

[65] Romans 12:2 "And do not be conformed to this world, but be transformed by the renewing of your

75

commands transformation through the renewal of the mind.

Be Anxious for Nothing

It is time to look at Philippians 4:6-9. These four verses form the foundation of *The Train* model. In this passage, Paul addresses the negative emotion of anxiety, but his methodology applies to anger and guilt as well. Paul begins with the simple command, "Be anxious for nothing." The NASB translates the Greek word *merimnao* as "anxious" in Philippians 4:6. *Merimnao* has the same usage as the English word "concern." Concern is anxiety, worry, or apprehension about the future. It involves an uncertainty about the good to come in the future. Anxiety matches our definition of fear, an uncertain expectation. Essentially anxiety is a mild version of fear.

The Scripture regularly warns against fear, worry, and anxiety. In Matthew 6:31, Jesus commands, "Do not be anxious then, saying, 'What shall we eat?' or 'What shall we drink?' or 'With what shall we clothe ourselves?'" 1 John 4:18 says that "perfect loves casts out fear." Jesus in Matthew 10:28 explains that no one should "fear man who can kill the body." The Bible specifically says either "do not be afraid" or "do not fear" 105 times. Clearly, fear does not belong in the Christian's life.

In Philippians 4:6-9, Paul gives the often-quoted advice, "Be anxious for nothing..." Jesus used the word *"merimna"* six times in Matthew 6:25-34 as He tells the disciples to not be anxious about food, clothing, shelter, or tomorrow. The word comes from a root which means "distracted." Anxiety is a distraction from faith. In Philippians 4, Paul explains how to remove anxiety from one's life.

Own Your Emotions

The first step is an honest evaluation of the heart. "Be anxious for nothing but in everything by prayer..." Paul's thought could be simplified by saying, "don't be afraid but pray." This raises the question, "pray for what?" The answer is to pray for the situation causing the anxiety. The first step in dealing with anxiety

---

mind, so that you may prove what the will of God is, that which is good and acceptable and perfect."

is to acknowledge the presence of anxiety. In order to free yourself from anxiety you have to admit that you are anxious. You have to begin with what "is" true before you can reach what "should" be true.

This is where many Christians fail. They know that they should not be anxious or afraid; therefore, they assert that they are not. A pastor once confronted a friend who had acted in a hurtful way toward him. As he confronted this individual with her sin, the offender replied, "I could not have done that because if I had, it would have been sin." The pastor continued to help his friend face her sin, but soon discovered the barrier that was preventing her repentance and reconciliation. This friend went on to honestly admit that she did not want to be forgiven. She wanted to be vindicated. Too often people want to be *right*, which is different than saying they want to *act righteously*. They do not want to fail. They are afraid that failure will make them less valuable or less lovable. This makes sense when you think about how most relationships work.

Some families have a certain tidal element to their relationships. Members of the family do something that offends another member. Rather than acting in grace toward one another, the offended party gets mad and stops speaking to the offender. This continues for a few weeks or months, or sometimes years. Eventually the offended party forgets the offense and begins speaking to the offender again as if nothing had ever happened. This all continues until another offense occurs. Then the whole cycle begins again.

You may think, "That only happens in highly dysfunctional families." Obviously, this cycle is a symptom of dysfunctionality, but it is more common than you might think. Any pastor will witness mild versions of this in their church. Christians demonstrate their displeasure with someone's actions in many different ways. These expressions of displeasure simply confirm the fears of the offender that they do not really measure up. They understand that forgiveness is not the value held in the Church: perfection is. That is why the number one complaint about

Christianity by non-Christians is that Christians are hypocrites or have holier-than-thou attitudes. The world sees that Christians frequently shun those who fail instead of forgiving them and leading them to reconciliation.

This leaves many in the Church with a sense that they need to be right and not mess up. So they begin their self-evaluation with what "should" be true and assert that it "*is*" true. They know they should be honest. They also know that if they are not quite honest, their friends will think poorly of them. Therefore, they assert that they always tell the whole truth and then simply ignore the white lies. This form of pretending isolates individuals from the power of the gospel. People do not seek forgiveness for sin but instead vindication of their actions. Honestly admitting fear is vital because repentance requires a specific sin from which to turn. Paul had this in mind when in Philippians 4:6 he invited Christians to acknowledge their fear and own its sinfulness. Christians must own the fact that they are afraid, and then they can take their fear to God in prayer with thanksgiving and supplication.

An honest assessment of your fear is important on another and far more important level. Fear is a sin. If you do not acknowledge your sin, you cannot be trusting Jesus to forgive that sin. He may have forgiven you as He forgives your sins of ignorance (Psalm 19:12).[66] However, you are not living in that forgiveness which would promote in you the thankfulness that Paul mentions in Philippians 4:6.

1 John 1:9 says, "If we confess our sins, He is faithful and righteous to forgive us our sins and to cleanse us from all unrighteousness." John reminds his readers that they do not need to be afraid to admit their sins because God is faithful and righteous to forgive. Like the little child who is tempted to lie about eating the cookie his mother told him not to eat, people are tempted to lie to God and pretend they have not sinned. Do not be afraid when you come to Him with your sin. Know that He will forgive you.

---

[66] Psalms 19:12 "Who can discern his errors? Acquit me of hidden faults."

In addition, confession is necessary to bring cleansing. Cleansing is the removal of sin from your life. Another name for that is repentance. If two people meet for lunch and one of them has a mustard stain on her shirt, the friend will likely notice it and immediately forgive it (after the appropriate amount of teasing about being sloppy). However, this forgiveness does not change; or clean the shirt. Cleansing occurs when the mustard is removed from the shirt. 1 John says that confession leads to repentance. You cannot repent of a sin that you do not acknowledge. Owning your sin before God sets you free to remove it from your life.

Search your heart. What are you feeling? Be honest and bring it openly to God, knowing that Jesus can handle any sin in your life. As you are honest, you will taste the beginnings of transformation. Paul says, "And the peace that surpasses comprehension shall guard your hearts and minds in Christ Jesus." This does not end your efforts to remove anxiety from your life. There is more.

Think Truth

In Philippians 4:8, Paul continues. "Whatever is true...let your mind dwell on these things." Removing negative emotions begins with an honest assessment of one's emotions. Change requires that the mind be engaged. Once honest admission of negative emotions has occurred, the mind must be disciplined to think truth. Paul treats the mind as the starting place for change. He gives a list of positive virtues that should fill the mind: truth, honor, rightness, purity, loveliness, good reputation, excellence, and praise-worthiness are all virtues deserving contemplation. At the head of this list is truth.

You are not afraid because you are in a dangerous situation, but because you are not thinking truth. If nothing can separate you from the love of God and God is all that you need, then there is no need to be afraid. If you wrongly think that you need to continue your time on this planet with the people you can see and feel, then a man pointing a gun at you is a terrifying experience. Fear, or anxiety, is directly tied to the untruth that an individual is thinking. Therefore, Paul says that in order to remove anxiety, people need to fill their minds with truth.

An individual facing these negative emotions usually needs to think truth on two levels. The first and most obvious level is that the individual must know that God is all that he needs. The second is that the individual needs to see God's love revealed through the situations and people around him. Consider the following composite sketch of a man coming to grips with these two levels of truth.

Dale is sitting in his car fuming at his wife Sara. Ten minutes ago, Sara asked him about their finances. Shortly after they were married, Dale wrote a few bad checks. He also ran up some debt on their credit cards. His mismanagement created a lot of difficulties for them. Dale learned from those situations, but he is still embarrassed by his failure. As soon as Sara started asking questions, he assumed that she was accusing him of failing again. Dale loves Sara, and her opinion of him matters. He wants to be a man that Sara can trust fully. He is afraid that she does not trust him to care for the finances. He is also terrified that, maybe, he is not worthy of her trust.

Believing that he needs Sara to respect him, Dale chooses to take offense at her lack of trust. Rather than allowing himself to be vulnerable to his wife's apparent concern which could bring either correction to his failure or comfort to her fearful heart, Dale responds with anger. His anger is aimed at preventing Sara from questioning his competence. Much like a dog protecting a bone, he growls to warn his wife that she should back away from this area of his life.

Notice that Dale has forgotten the truth that all he needs is for God to respect him. His desire for Sara's respect has become an expectation. It is not a proper expectation since he has no control over it. Sara blocked his expectation by not demonstrating trust in the way Dale wanted, and he became angry. When Dale perceives that Sara is withholding from him his desperate need for respect, he responds with anger. On a second level, it is very likely that Sara *does* respect Dale. She may have several good reasons to ask about the finances. She may be planning a surprise party and wants to know how much to spend. It is possible that she is fearful because of Dale's past failures. She may want to put her fears to rest by knowing the truth of their money situation. Her questions provide Dale with the opportunity to demonstrate his competence with their finances. The fact is that she respects Dale very much. Sadly, Dale refuses to see her trust because he has chosen to think and believe untruth. Ironically, he does not trust his wife to trust him.

Untruth is magnetic. It collects other untruths to itself with lightning speed. Dale begins by thinking he needs Sara's respect. He quickly moves to the assumption that she does not respect him. To this untruth is added the thought that she is accusing him of mismanaging the finances which leads him to conclude that she thinks he is incompetent as a husband and therefore as a man. It is ugly how the snowball collects all of these lies and drives a wedge separating the man and his wife (Matthew 19:6[67]). It seems almost diabolical. It may very well be. The devil is called the accuser of the brethren. Maybe he is whispering some of these accusations. It is important for us to remember this reality when caring for couples in crisis.

Dale needs to focus his mind on truth. The truth is that even if Sara does not respect him, he is okay. He does not need to be respected by anyone but God. He should instead focus on living a respectable life. If he has failed in the finances, he should change his practice. If he has not, he should serve Sara by allowing her full access to their financial information. In addition, Dale should stop and remember that Sara is a sinful person. She might be struggling with her fears. Instead of protecting himself, he has the opportunity to reach out to her in her weakness and comfort her. Sara's fear actually provides him with the opportunity to protect his wife. Finally, Dale should remember Sara's past expressions of love and trust for him. Such an exercise will fill his mind with the truth that will remove his fear and anger.

---

[67] Matthew 19:6 "So they are no longer two, but one flesh. What therefore God has joined together, let no man separate."

Do the Right Thing

Look at the last section of Philippians 4:6-9. The Apostle Paul's first exhortation is to acknowledge one's emotions. The second step is to fill one's mind with truth. Paul is very aware that just thinking something does not make it so. The Christian must put the truth into action. Therefore, he writes in verse 9, "The things you have learned and received and heard and seen in me, practice these things; and the God of peace shall be with you." The final step is to engage the will and live the truth that now fills the mind.

Once a person begins to fill her mind with truth, she needs to put it into practice. Paul says, "...practice these things." All of the commands of Scripture are summarized with the command to love. Romans 13:10 says, "Love does no wrong to a neighbor; love therefore is the fulfillment of the law." Jesus summarized the law with two commands: to love God and to love your neighbor (Matthew 22:37-39).[68] "How can I act in love in this situation?" becomes the predominant question to answer. The focus is not on being loved, which is passive and consequently outside of my control, but on loving other people.

Think again about Dale, the slightly insecure husband. His motives are self-protecting. He is not interested in ministering to his wife. He is consumed by the drive to make Sara meet his needs. In his mind, she has threatened his need for respect. He is not, at that moment, loving her. When he fills his mind with the two truths that God meets his needs and Sara respects him, he is set free to love Sara (John 8:32).[69] Knowing that God respects him, he is able to express Jesus' love for her (Ephesians 5:25-27).[70] He is able to pursue the highest good possible in her life, which is faith in the love of Jesus Christ. He can only pursue her good when he is convinced of his own personal safety. When Dale steps into this

---

[68] Matthew 22:37-39 And He said to him, " 'You shall love the Lord your God with all your heart, and with all your soul, and with all your mind.' 38 "This is the great and foremost commandment. 39 "The second is like it, 'You shall love your neighbor as yourself.'

[69] John 8:32 "and you will know the truth, and the truth will make you free."

[70] Ephesians 5:25-27 "Husbands, love your wives, just as Christ also loved the church and gave Himself up for her, 26 so that He might sanctify her, having cleansed her by the washing of water with the word, 27 that He might present to Himself the church in all her glory, having no spot or wrinkle or any such thing; but that she would be holy and blameless."

freedom, remembering the truth and acting in love, he experiences that "the God of peace is with him."

Summary

Philippians 4:6-9 gives a helpful flow of transformation. The model of *The Train* is a visual representation of this path to transformation. An individual feels a negative emotion and admits it to God in prayer with thanksgiving, trusting the forgiveness Jesus provides (vv. 6-7). He then takes time to fill his mind with truth, seeking to adopt God's perspective on the situation (v. 8). Finally, with his mind armed with truth, he steps out in faith, peacefully convinced of God's presence so that he can actively love the people around him, setting them free to experience the love of Jesus in a fresh way (v. 9).

7 SHIELDS

After these things the word of the Lord came to Abram in a vision,
saying,
"Do not fear, Abram,
I am a shield to you;
Your reward shall be very great."
Genesis 15:1

In 1990, during the early morning hours, a man broke into my mother's apartment, held a knife to her throat, mocked her, threatened her, and raped her. Although he left her alive, something in my mother died that day.

Throughout her life, Mom has been a victim of abuse. Her father abused her verbally and physically. When she met my father she saw her chance to escape. On her eighteenth birthday they were married. She soon discovered that he was even worse. She would try to anticipate his wishes to avoid his rage, but who can know the whims of a drunken man. After an exceptionally brutal beating, Mom expressed her truest self when she courageously gathered her three sons and left my dad. I thank God for her courage. That choice has always been an example to me that I do not need to live under oppression and it set me free from living any longer under my father's wrath. She left with another man and soon married him. Although not as violent as my father, he too drank too much and would often act in oppressive ways. The relief was so great that we overlooked his controlling ways and periodic fits of rage.

When I was ten, my step-father took his own life. He got mad about something we boys had done. He fought with mom and she took us to her mother's for our safety. The next morning, she called Grandma and told her that he had killed himself. We were stunned. I remember vividly the numbness that fell over our whole family. Even in this state, Mom brought us all together. She was a rock. She was brave and strong. I admire my mom for the amazing power she showed to raise three teenage boys all alone. But in one night in January 1990, Mom became frightened. Maybe it was the straw the broke the camel's back. I do not know for sure. But Mom has been different ever since.

Because of the rape, Mom married a man who would be the worst of her abusers. He offered her safety from the intruder. In exchange, he demanded total obedience. One day when he felt she was slipping away, he pointed a pistol at her chest and squeezed the trigger. In God's grace, the weapon misfired and Mom was able to escape. Two months later, Mom met Jesus. Her faith has set her free from so much destruction. Although she has regained some of her fearless confidence, she still longs to be safe. She is afraid of unlocked doors. She winces when she sees someone who is similar to her attacker. I admire my Mom and I weep for the burden she must carry. I do not blame my mom for being afraid. I would love for her to be fully free, but I understand that her wounds are greater than anything I can even imagine. She is fighting just to survive. How can a man sunbathing on the beach criticize the swimming technique of the survivor of a shipwreck who is struggling against the tide to reach the shore? Mom is worthy of my admiration.

A member of my church, Janice, once confided in me, "Vince, you know how deeply the rape affected your mom. You know that that single violent act scarred her for life." I nodded. "I was raped every day for years by my step-father." What do you say to such a revelation? How do you even understand the wounds this woman bore? To this day, I am deeply grateful that my friend is still alive. She is struggling to be a better mother and wife. She has not given up the fight but as she walks through this life, she has a noticeable limp. The wounds inflicted by her step-father will be with her throughout this life.

Bruises

Each of us is wounded in life. Our wounds may not reach the severity of Mom's or Janice's, but we have been hurt. Mom and Janice live, trying to find some way to be safe from the wounds they experienced. Their methods are different. Their fears are slightly different, but their primary objective is the same. They cannot bear the possibility that someone might hurt them again.

Lee Cox, in his book *Raised on Fear,* tells of his own struggles to overcome the fear that defined him. During an argument with his girlfriend, she pointed out something that he had done which was wrong. Lee turned over the table and swore at her in his rage. He recognized that when she pointed out that he was wrong, he anticipated that he would be punished just as his father used to punish him, with severe beatings and demeaning insults. Lee could not bear such punishment, so he lashed out to protect himself from what he anticipated but could not bear.

> At times like these, when I was feeling really good about what a great guy I was, I was most vulnerable to criticism. At the instant I heard I was "wrong" or "bad" I went from feeling great to feeling like the worst person on the planet. Being wrong meant I needed to be punished, and I was not aware of anything except that I had to stop her from hurting me. I saw myself as justified in whatever it took to stop her. I did feel bad afterwards, but not like I had done something wrong, just that she had forced me into protecting myself that much. I actually hated Marian for hurting me.[71]

How does someone face life after such pain? They must find something to shield them from the pain. Most of the time, people learn to build and trust self-protective strategies. Lee Cox used his anger to protect himself. Many victims of abuse use the same

---

[71]Lee Cox, *Raised on Fear* (Milltown, EVE Foundation, 2004) 68.

abusive tactics with which they had been oppressed to protect themselves from the oppression they fear. There are many different strategies people adopt and use based on their experience and the severity of the perceived threat. It seems heartless to encourage a wounded person to drop their guard, but although these strategies are understandable, each one is actually self-destructive. Each self-protective strategy replaces Jesus as the individual's shield, protector, and mediator.

In 2006, I was playing a pickup game of basketball. I came down with a rebound surrounded by two other players. My foot landed partially on one another player's foot and rolled. Because I was pinned between two players, I could not fall to the side. The result was a severely damaged ankle. The recovery would take around a year. Even after the ankle was healed, I remember being nervous when anything got too close to my ankle, especially when it was a sudden movement. It was over a year before I would wear sandals again. Even today, eight years later, I am a little hesitant walking down steep hills. My injury affected the way I live. I am much more cautious and overly protective of my ankle. Sometimes, my caution is unnecessary, maybe even irrational.

As people experience emotional pain in life they become protective as well. We can call these emotional wounds "bruises." When someone has a bruise, they wince whenever anything approaches the bruise. Although they do not consciously think about the bruise, they are continually aware of it and act to keep it safe. In one's effort to protect their emotional bruises they can build lifelong self-protective patterns that are unhealthy, preventing their growth and effectiveness in reaching others.

Shields

Think about self-protective strategies as shields. The purpose of a shield is to come between you and a dangerous weapon. Recently, the terror group, Hamas, was accused of using human shields in Gaza. They fire their missiles into Israel from schools and hospitals, trusting that Israel will not return fire on a school. Hamas trusts children, injured people, sick people and care-givers to stand between them and the Israeli bombs. In ages past, war was predominantly fought hand to hand. In such a battle, it was important to carry an offensive weapon (such as a sword) and a shield to block the enemy's blows. The warrior would hide behind his shield awaiting a moment of safety so that he could strike against the enemy.

People use self-protective strategies in exactly this way. First, they believe that they are at war. They see the world around them as dangerous and the people around them as threats. Instead of seeing the needs around them and responding to God's call to care for others, they lift their shield of self-protective strategies. People see the world in this way because they have been attacked. The crowd expresses displeasure at people who do not follow the crowd. Maybe the crowd laughs at them, communicating that they do not measure up. The crowd may mock the non-conformist, get angry at them, or physically harm them. In each of these situations the non-conformist's value is challenged and their safety removed. It seems that it is safer to assume people are dangerous, than to risk such harm. (Isn't that the point of "stranger danger"? Because some children have been harmed by strangers, people teach their children to be afraid of every stranger. While providing safety to children, it also prevents truly loving people from expressing love to the children.)

Not only do people live as if they are at war but they hide behind their shields. Many use conformity as a shield. As long as an individual fits in, she will not be attacked. She may use charm or anger, buying gifts or being needy, cynicism or Pollyanna style optimism to avoid the attacks. Many people resort to books like *How to Win Friends and Influence People* as a shield to help them win in the warfare of this life. Others seek to control everything around them. These become the abusers, whose shield is an effort to control life so that it will not hurt them again. They justify their actions, often blinded to their abuse, but in the end they are hiding behind a shield.

The Apostle Paul talks about shields in Ephesians 6:11-17.

Put on the full armor of God, so that you will be able to stand firm against the schemes of the devil.

> For our struggle is not against flesh and blood, but against the rulers, against the powers, against the world forces of this darkness, against the spiritual *forces* of wickedness in the heavenly *places*. Therefore, take up the full armor of God, so that you will be able to resist in the evil day, and having done everything, to stand firm. Stand firm therefore, HAVING GIRDED YOUR LOINS WITH TRUTH, and HAVING PUT ON THE BREASTPLATE OF RIGHTEOUSNESS, and having shod YOUR FEET WITH THE PREPARATION OF THE GOSPEL OF PEACE; in addition to all, taking up the shield of faith with which you will be able to extinguish all the flaming arrows of the evil *one*. And take THE HELMET OF SALVATION, and the sword of the Spirit, which is the word of God.

He begins by reminding his readers that their battle is not against people but against the evil one. As people use their time strategizing about the people around them, they miss the real issue. While they are supposed to be reaching out to others with love, people are busy hiding behind their shields ready for the next attack. And the world is perishing around them.

When Paul speaks of the Christian's shield, he calls it the "shield of faith." How is faith a shield? Peter may enlighten us as to that question. He says that Jesus endured the hostility of crucifixion by "entrusting Himself to the one who judges righteously.[72]" Jesus believed that His Father would care for Him. He knew that even if He died, He would live because His Father had promised. His faith "extinguished all the flaming arrows of the evil one." Peter tells Christians to follow Jesus in this trusting of the Father. It is better to be comforted by Jesus than to avoid pain (Matthew 5:4[73], 11:28-30[74]). One may acknowledge this in

---

[72] 1 Peter 2:23-24 "and while being reviled, He did not revile in return; while suffering, He uttered no threats, but kept entrusting Himself to Him who judges righteously..."

[73] Matthew 5:4 "Blessed are those who mourn, for they shall be comforted."

[74] Matthew 11:28-30 "Come to Me, all who are weary and heavy-laden, and I will give you rest. 29 "Take My yoke upon you and learn from Me, for I am gentle and humble in heart, and you will find rest for your souls. 30 "For My yoke is easy and My burden is light."

his mind; however it is faith that makes the Father's care into a shield. Believing in the nearness of God and His sole ability to meet one's needs extinguishes the flaming arrows of the crowd's disapproval. They lose their power in one's life.

Identify Strategies

You have likely heard of the Napoleon complex, or short man syndrome. It is the idea that a man under 5' 9" will try harder than taller men in order to compensate for their sense of inferiority due to height.[75] While this can be a generalization, the reality is that some short men do try harder. This is a self-protective strategy that brings some good into their lives. While this strategy may provide the drive to accomplish important tasks, it also drives people away. It hides a deep insecurity and leads the individual to pretend to be more. This person is afraid that shortness may define them. Therefore they create an elaborate facade to hide their perceived weakness.

Often, one's shields are not as helpful as they would hope. They provide some semblance of control over life, but they also build barriers between an individual and others that prevent them from receiving the intense love of God and from impacting the lives around them. These shields, which people hope will protect them, become the instruments that disrupt their relationships and prevent them from accomplishing God's will.

Therefore, Christians need to learn what shields they have built and what bruises they protect. By identifying these shields they can take their wounds directly to Jesus for healing. The Christian can know that he may have to walk around with scars from the previous wounds; he may be wounded again, but he is committed to go to Jesus with his pains.

Ellen is a warm and friendly woman. If you were to visit her church, she would likely be one of the first to greet you. She genuinely loves people, and she shows it. She often reaches out to new people and begins to build a quick bond. She will call a

---

[75] Stanley Loewen, Health Guidance, http://www.healthguidance.org/entry/15851/1/Short-Man-Syndrome-Explained.html, accessed 04/21/2015

couple of times each week, initiate meetings and pray for her new friend. This lasts for a few months and then Ellen meets a new friend. Just as quickly as it started the relationship seems to end. She is investing in someone new. Ellen does not even see this pattern.

Why does she do this? Ellen, like many others, enjoys newness, but there is more. When Ellen was eight, her best friend was Susie. They spent all of their time together and shared their secrets. One day Susie broke their confidence and told another girl one of Ellen's most treasured secrets. Ellen was embarrassed and betrayed. Most adults could deal with this quite easily but for an eight-year-old it was devastating. Ellen knew that she should not have trusted Susie. She would not let anyone get that close again. Thus began her life of many relationships.

We all have shields. What are yours?

When Maya Angelou was young, she was raped by her mother's boyfriend. She told her brother who told the rest of the family. The man was arrested, convicted and then incarcerated for one day. Four days after his release, he was murdered—it is believed by Maya's uncles. Maya felt responsible. She felt that her act of telling her brother cost the man his life. She did not speak again for four years. Her wound led to the errant idea that she was responsible for this man's death. She was not rational—due in part to the trauma—failing to see that his crime cost him his life. As a small child, she had to process all of this emotion. She jumped to the conclusion that she caused his death with her words, so she quit speaking. Imagine how impoverished this world would be, if Maya Angelou had never spoken again. That is what her shield would have produced, *but God...*

Section 2: Implementing the Principles

VINCENT L. WOOD

8 NOW WHAT?

What use is it, my brethren, if a man says he has faith, but he has
no works? Can that faith save him? If a brother or sister is without
clothing and in need of daily food, and one of you says to them,
"Go in peace, be warmed and be filled," and yet you do not give
them what is necessary for their body, what use is that? Even so
faith, if it has no works, is dead, being by itself.
James 2:14-17

    Lee loved Michelle deeply. When he started to date her, he
left all of his friends. Even his family had become less important to
him. He would spend as much time with her as he could. He felt
so alive when she was near him. Michelle loved Lee and treated
him with great respect and kindness. Their wedding day was the
happiest day of their lives.

    One morning, Lee was sitting in a coffee shop for his
weekly meeting with Del. Del was helping Lee deal with his grief.
One year ago, Michelle had been shot and killed in a parking lot.
She was a random victim of a mugger who got scared.

    "I remember how terrified I used to get when she would go
to Bible study on Thursday nights. I would walk outside and watch
for her car. I trembled with fear as I imagined her suffering
through a kidnapping, or being in a fatal car accident. I would
pray, but my prayers were more like primal screams for help than

real communication with God. This happened every week. I couldn't stand for her to go anywhere alone. I wanted to be with her to protect her. The idea of living without Michelle was overwhelming. I don't think I ever put it into words, but I knew Michelle was the only person who really loved me and saw me as a good person. I knew that my fear was wrong. I tried to pretend that it wasn't that bad, but inside, I knew that I was not trusting God to take care of her.

"Del, on the night Michelle was killed, I asked her to go to the store for me. We had a rule that she would not go to the store at night without me. It was just another way that I tried to protect her. Maybe, it was more about protecting me. Anyway, I was so sick that day, and we were out of cold medicine. I needed something, so I asked her to go to the store. She was there in the parking lot because of me. I failed to protect her. In fact, I sent her out, and she got killed. I feel like such a worthless man. I was so weak that I could not even love my wife enough to go to the store for my own stupid medicine. Instead, I sent a helpless woman out to a dangerous place where she was killed. Oh, God, I feel awful."

A football coach, filled with enthusiasm and a love for the game, gathers a group of kids together to make a football team. He carefully describes each position to the kids. He instructs them on all of the fundamentals of the sport from blocking, to throwing, to tackling. He even helps the kids to understand proper time management on the field. He is convinced that he has given the kids all of the information they need to be a successful football team.

The first game arrives, and the coach, excited to see the kids use what he has taught them, sends them out onto the field with the words, "Now go do it!"

The team looks at their coach with bewilderment. "Do what, Coach?"

"Everything I've taught you."

The kids are at a loss. They wonder, "When and whom shall I block? When do I throw the ball? Who throws the ball?" Again they ask, "What do we do?"

The enthusiastic coach did a wonderful job of explaining the pieces to the kids. However, he failed to connect the pieces. He needed to apply the fundamentals to specific situations. He needed to give the kids a game plan and instruct them as they tried to follow it. This chapter is our game plan. How does we use the information presented in this book to bring real change in real situations?

The Goal

The goal of ministry is to help people rest fully in God. The temptation to help people feel better is very real and almost irresistible. When a woman comes to a pastor and explains how her husband relentlessly yells at her and demeans her every action, he will want to help her by making him stop. It feels heartless to do anything else. But this is not our job. Our job is not to provide her with tools to control or manipulate her husband's behavior. We should teach her how to rest in Christ even in the midst of hardship. That is not to suggest that the abused woman should remain in the home or even in the abusive relationship. But she can never make it her objective to control another person. The supreme example is the Lord Jesus. 1 Peter 2:21-23 says,

> 21 For you have been called for this purpose, since Christ also suffered for you, leaving you an example for you to follow in His steps, 22 who committed no sin, nor was any deceit found in His mouth; 23 and while being reviled, He did not revile in return; while suffering, He uttered no threats, but kept entrusting Himself to Him who judges righteously.

Verse 21 says to follow Jesus' example. In verses 22-23, Peter explains exactly what that example is. We are to face abuse and hardship by continually entrusting ourselves to the "one who judges righteously." What we need to do is help everyone who comes to us move toward such trust in God.

God values endurance. Think about Romans 5:3-5. "And not only this, but we also exult in our tribulations, knowing that tribulation brings about perseverance; and perseverance, proven character; and proven character, hope; and hope does not disappoint…" Endurance produces hope. James 1:3 tells us to "consider it all joy" when we face hardship. Hardship produces endurance. Too often we are tempted to help people avoid hardship instead of equipping them to endure it. When we provide counsel that seeks to remove difficult circumstances from a person's life, we have set aside the Word of God, and we are seeking an objective which is inconsistent with God's revealed will.

Most people try to help because they care about people. Their love for people drives them to want to help people feel better. We must stay focused on helping people *get* better, not merely *feel* better. What the hurting person needs is Jesus Christ and *nothing else*. He is the source of all satisfaction. Every person is made for Him and can only find their fulfillment in a relationship with Him. So we must bring people to Jesus, strengthening their faith that He is sufficient for all they need. This is real help.

In his book *Effective Biblical Counseling*, Dr. Larry Crabb describes the goal of counseling as, "*to free people to better worship and serve God* by helping them become more like the Lord. In a word, the goal is maturity.[76]" The objective of all Christian ministry is always maturity: a greater faith in the Lord and His work in our life.

The Train

Another concept that should direct our efforts is that the heart works like a train. The mind is the engine. The emotions are responses to a person's thinking. We must address the mind, filling it with truth in order to bring about new strategies for relating to people and situations in life. These right strategies, based on truth, will produce God-honoring emotional responses. The emotions always follow the choices an individual makes,

---

[76] Lawrence J. Crabb, *Effective Biblical Counseling*, (Grand Rapids, Zondervan 1977) 22.

which are always based on his perception of truth.

By following *The Train* paradigm, we set individuals free to control their own emotions. It makes each person responsible for his own anger, fear, and guilt, while at the same time providing the pathway for true righteousness. We must work to set people free. Jesus said, "The truth will set you free."[77] Focusing energy on the engine (the mind) and then directing the will with the implications of the truth will bring transformation.

Identify and Define the Emotions

Emotions are responses to the success of strategies to meet perceived needs. Success brings positive emotions. Failure or potential failure brings negative feelings. Most people do not believe this. A struggling person believes that his emotion is right, given his circumstance. He believes that situations outside of his control have created these negative emotions, and he wants those situations changed. He wants someone to teach him how to successfully alter the people and circumstances in his life. If his child is rebellious, he will want you to teach him how to control his child. If her husband is distant, she will want you to show her how to win his affections. If God feels distant, he will want you to help him feel God's presence. What he wants is to feel better fast. You may not be able to oblige.

Shortly after a young man went to college, he called his father to seek advice about his car. He said that it made a strange sound sometimes when he stopped or went over a bump. The father told him that it might be the brakes. His mother visited to shuttle him around while the car was being fixed. She called shortly after she arrived and mentioned that his brake light was flashing. That clarified the problem. The father asked his son, "How long has the light been flashing?" "A couple of weeks." "Did it seem significant to you that the light was flashing?" It had not occurred to him that the flashing light and the sound were connected.

In the same way, most people do not even consider that

---

[77] John 8:32 "and you will know the truth, and the truth will make you free."

their emotions are the result of their own wrong thinking. They choose to cover up the warning light with duct tape and proceed on their merry way, unaware that a "blow-up" is imminent. As we invest in others, we must begin with the assumption that one's emotions can be trusted. They can be trusted to reveal that something is wrong in one's thinking and in their choices. The problem lies *within* each person, not *around* them. We can help individuals look inside and see their own flawed thinking as the source of their emotional distress. Identifying and defining the specific emotions is essential to discovering and changing one's wrong thoughts.

Anger

Anger is a *blocked expectation*. In the will people build desires and expectations. Both of these are faith-driven. People desire what they believe is good. They develop expectations around what they believe they need. Desires are not tied to our needs, but to our wants. Unmet desires produce disappointment but not emotional distress. Anger reveals that the loss experienced is not of a desire but an expectation, something the individual believes she needs.

An expectation is tied to the sense of need. Because a person needs to be loved, they expect other people to express love to them. If a person does not have an unconditionally accepting relationship, and if that person does not have a valuable purpose in this life, they are ruined. The options are: love and value, or destruction. Therefore, everyone expects their needs to be met. Where my thinking misleads my faith is when I think and believe that I need someone other than God to meet these needs. Therefore, anger reveals that someone or something has disrupted my plan to be loved or valued. Anger serves as a warning that I have wandered away from believing that God is all that I need. If I trust the message that my anger is giving me, I can quickly return to my Savior.

Many people find value in their work. At work a person is significant to the extent that they are competent. This conviction begins in childhood when people are praised for good grades or for being good at sports. When they won the Spelling Bee, everyone made a huge deal about it. When they took fourth, they heard, "You'll do better next time." People long for affirming words, and they realize that the winner is the most valuable. It is easy to believe that one's value is not the individual expression of God's character that each person possesses, but it is found in doing the "greatest" things: in being better than others. This means that our value is found in relation to others rather than in relation to God. This errant conviction is carried into the work environment. Believing that one must be competent, a person begins to expect the people at work to treat them as a competent person. This may require one to work extremely long hours to do the best job possible. The respect that his co-workers offer is an affirmation that he is indeed valuable. People subtly make their fellow workers the source of their sense of significance. The co-workers are now, in effect, god: the one who meets one's needs.

As long as a person does not show any incompetence, and the co-workers continue to demonstrate appreciation for his success, he is satisfied. However, when the moment comes that the worker fails, and the boss yells at him in front of the other employees, his world begins to crumble. Not only must he now face his failure, but he must also face the public scorn of his peers. His expectation has now been shattered by the boss's harsh words and public revelation of his failure. His expectation of being respected by his peers has been blocked, so he responds in what he feels is an appropriate fashion, with anger. He is angry at the boss's choice to berate him publicly. He will likely build shields. He may justify his worth by demonstrating how the boss is wrong. He may hide behind an ad-hominem argument asserting that the boss is just mean. He may take a faux-humble approach and gain sympathy from his co-workers. In each of these situations he is fighting to maintain a sense of value.

Here is how one shield might develop. For illustration purposes, call the worker Jim. Initially Jim's anger is tied directly to his loss of respect. Jim wonders what people will think of him. He is too smart to leave it there. Jim knows it is a sign of weakness to care what other people think. So with a deft assertion,

Jim declares that the problem is that the boss made the correction public. As a Christian, Jim turns to Matthew 18 and points out that the boss should have come to Jim privately. Jim's self-centered anger is now a "righteous indignation." Lost in the whole scenario is the fact that Jim failed in the first place. Jim easily set aside his own failure and focused on the failure of the boss. In this way, Jim insulated himself from facing the real issue: a lack of faith in the sufficiency of Jesus. Jim's anger was a kind reminder by God that he had begun to raise other people and their opinion of him to the place that God alone should hold as the Giver of Jim's value.

A simple shift would have changed this whole situation. If Jim had recognized his anger as a blocked expectation, an indication that his heart was wrong, then Jim could have humbly heard the boss and faced his personal failure. In owning his failure, Jim not only could have corrected it, but he could also have spoken words of life into his boss's life. Consider the witnessing opportunity that is missed because of Jim's anger. Instead of willingly facing his flaws, as the cross of Jesus allows him to do, he acted in a self-righteous fashion. Self-righteousness, also known as hypocrisy, is the greatest obstacle most non-Christians face to believing in Jesus. Instead of providing a declaration of the sufficiency of Jesus to provide forgiveness and empower repentance, Jim declared that he had to get it right or at least pretend to get it right. That is too bad and too frequent. And it is all because Jim did not listen to the reminder of God which was his emotion of anger.

Anger is a blocked expectation. Chapter four defined a proper expectation as "any legitimate want over which one has total control." We can conclude that a blocked expectation is an improper expectation. If someone can block an expectation, it must not be totally in one's control. All proper expectations rely entirely on one's self to accomplish them. When a person feels the beginnings of anger, or frustration, they must look at their own heart and identify their expectation. They must not only name it, they must confess it as sin (1 John 1:9) and take steps to remove it from their life.

Fear

Fear is an *uncertain expectation*. It occurs when a person is not completely confident that his expectation will be met. Knowing that he needs to be loved and valued, he chooses desires and expectations to meet these needs. Once again, people tend to set these expectations on the people and circumstances around them. Rather than trusting the invisible God (2 Corinthians 5:7)[78], people long to be loved by others whom they can see, hear, touch, and smell. People are not always interested in giving others the love and respect they need. When a person faces a situation in which they are not likely to receive love or respect, they become anxious, worried that their needs may not be met.

Consider the following illustration. Pastor Morris receives a report that one of the elders has been viewing pornography. He knows that he needs to confront the elder about this sin. This same elder, Mr. Billings, has been in disagreements with the pastor for the past couple of months. *(Such disagreements frequently accompany sexual sins.)* It seems that he opposes the direction Pastor Morris wants to lead the Church. These disagreements have not always been civil. Mr. Billings has been quite belligerent in his disagreements. The pastor has also seen some indications that the elder has taken his disagreements to other members of the congregation, disparaging the pastor in the process. And now, Pastor Morris needs to correct Mr. Billings for a sin that is terribly destructive. He has a knot in his stomach.

Why is Pastor Morris so anxious? The first inclination is to blame Mr. Billings. His angry words and slanderous actions prove that he is not safe. It appears to be right for the pastor to be afraid, but is it?

Process this situation through *The Train*. Pastor Morris' fear, like all fear, is an uncertain expectation. God has given him this anxiety as a warning signal that his thoughts are not true, and therefore his faith object at this moment is not Jesus Christ. He expects to have his needs met through his interaction with Mr. Billings. He forgot that God alone is all he needs. He likely

---

[78] 2 Corinthians 5:7 "for we walk by faith, not by sight."

expects to be respected by this member of his Church—which seems reasonable. This expectation is even stronger since this member is a colleague on the leadership team. Pastor Morris believes that he needs his elders to respect him. They should show this respect by trusting him as he leads the church and speaks into their lives. Mr. Billings has not demonstrated much trust in Pastor Morris lately. The pastor doubts if he will trust him now. His stomach hurts.

When Pastor Morris was a child his parents would often argue loudly. It was usually+ at night, and they thought he was asleep. However, he would hear them fight until one day, his father left the home. As a child, he had to process this heartbreaking life situation. He was convinced that arguing will end a relationship. He spent most of his life trusting his shield—to avoid conflict. But now his calling demands that he enter a confrontational situation. He cannot trust his shield to protect him. His stomach hurts.

Pastor Morris' stomach hurts because he is seeking for someone other than God to affirm his competence and unconditional acceptance. He will have to risk the possibility that he will lose this relationship. Such a risk feels like it may destroy him. Instead of entering this relationship with unconditional love for Mr. Billings, Pastor Morris is looking to get something from him. Pastor Morris' improper expectation, not the elder's sinful actions, is the cause of his fear. If Pastor Morris can remember and trust that He is God's man in this situation, perfectly prepared to speak to Mr. Billings about his sin, if he can remember just how deadly pornography is to this man whom he loves, and if he can act in faith on these propositions, then Pastor Morris will be free from fear and able to lovingly help his brother face his sin (Galatians 6:1-2).[79] His fear will subside when he fills his mind with truth and acts in faith upon that truth. He must stop looking to get from Mr. Billings and instead give his own life for the benefit of this brother (Philippians 2:17).[80]

---

[79] Galatians 6:1-2 "Brethren, even if anyone is caught in any trespass, you who are spiritual, restore such a one in a spirit of gentleness; each one looking to yourself, so that you too will not be tempted. 2 Bear one another's burdens, and thereby fulfill the law of Christ."

Guilt

Guilt is a difficult topic. Many will say, "Of course I feel guilty. I *am* guilty." While this fact is indisputable, it is also true that feeling guilty is more than an admission of personal culpability. More often it is a form of penance. People want to feel bad because they think it is somehow right to feel bad, even after they confess their sin and claim forgiveness. It is thought that feeling bad will promote future obedience. In question #87 the Westminster Shorter Catechism says, "Repentance unto life is a saving grace, whereby a sinner, out of a true sense of his sin, and apprehension of the mercy of God in Christ, doth, with grief and hatred of his sin, turn from it unto God..." Repentance does not occur simply when one sees how bad his sin is. He must also apprehend the mercy of God in Christ. It is "the kindness of God that leads you to repentance" (Romans 2:4).

Guilt is an *unreachable expectation*. It comes when one's expectation is to do something that is impossible. For some people it comes in the form of perfectionism. Perfectionism is a denial of the sufficiency of Jesus' work. The belief that one needs to get it right comes when the individual forgets that Jesus got it right for him. This is Paul's problem in 2 Corinthians 12:7-10:

> And because of the surpassing greatness of the revelations, for this reason, to keep me from exalting myself, there was given me a thorn in the flesh, a messenger of Satan to buffet me —to keep me from exalting myself! Concerning this I entreated the Lord three times that it might depart from me. And He has said to me, "My grace is sufficient for you, for power is perfected in weakness." Most gladly, therefore, I will rather boast about my weaknesses, that the power of Christ may dwell in me. Therefore I am well content with weaknesses, with insults, with distresses, with persecutions, with difficulties, for Christ's sake; for when I am weak, then I am strong.

---

[80] Philippians 2:17 "But even if I am being poured out as a drink offering upon the sacrifice and service of your faith, I rejoice and share my joy with you all."

Paul was a Pharisee. The Pharisees believed that they had to obey perfectly in order to be accepted by God. They subsequently codified life to such an extent that they could feel comfortable that they had always obeyed. All of Paul's life, before salvation, was devoted to his own personal obedience. This same devotion made him uncommonly judgmental. We see a touch of this judgmental spirit when he separates from Barnabas over John Mark (see Acts 15:36-39).[81]

Paul was distressed with his own failure—what he called a thorn in the flesh. This failure may have been his judgmental spirit. He pleads with God to take it away. Three separate times he is so vexed by this thorn that he begs God to just take it away. His old Pharisee may have been leading him to trust in his own obedience. However, God says to him, "Trust that my grace is enough." God's word, "My grace is sufficient for you," may have been on Paul's mind when he wrote to the Philippians of his desire to "… be found in Him, not having a righteousness of my own derived from the Law, but that which is through faith in Christ, the righteousness which comes from God on the basis of faith" (Philippians 3:9).

Sometimes a sense of guilt is not just before God but before people. One thinks he needs people to believe he is good. When he fails in front of them, he is racked with guilt. He feels awful that he has let someone else down. The unreachable expectation is that no one should ever see him fail. The proper expectation is that Jesus will never fail to forgive. Romans 8:1says, "There is therefore now no condemnation for those who are in Christ Jesus." The Christian must choose to believe this verse, leaving the feelings of personal failure at the foot of the cross, and receive the joy that Jesus provides. Guilt is removed by thinking and believing truth!

---

[81] Acts 15:36-39 "After some days Paul said to Barnabas, "Let us return and visit the brethren in every city in which we proclaimed the word of the Lord, and see how they are." Barnabas wanted to take John, called Mark, along with them also. But Paul kept insisting that they should not take him along who had deserted them in Pamphylia and had not gone with them to the work. And there occurred such a sharp disagreement that they separated from one another, and Barnabas took Mark with him and sailed away to Cyprus."

Idols of the Heart

What the emotions show is idolatry. Anger, fear and guilt all reveal that the individual feeling these emotions is looking to a false god to meet their deepest needs. That god may be family, friends, co-workers or even one's self. This fact must not be minimized. A "blocked expectation" does not fully capture the gravity of the situation. The idea that one is worshipping false gods more accurately reflects the real problem of anger, fear, and guilt. It is vital to remove these bad emotions from one's life. It is not just a matter of feeling better. The reason people feel awful is because they are violating the very fabric of their existence by turning away from the one true God to seek satisfaction in that which is by nature poisonous (Jeremiah 2:13).[82] Until a person grasps the gravity of the situation, she will mess around with pop-psychology and self-help techniques that never address the real issue. The issue is that she is an unfaithful follower of Jesus. Even Christians forget and choose to not trust that Jesus alone is the source of life. Our job is to bring people to the source; equipping them to trust Him even in the most difficult situations.

Summary

The Train is a paradigm that focuses our efforts in ministering to other believers. As people consider a specific life situation through *The Train*, they can identify the wrong choices and the wrong thinking that led to their feelings of anger, fear and guilt. Once people identify this wrong thinking, they are empowered to change. They can remember the truth and put their trust in Jesus as the only source of life. They can taste the joy which Jesus promises to those who truly trust Him. They are set free to fulfill the purpose God gave them; to love Him with all their heart, and to love their neighbor as themselves.

Instead of revealing how I would help Lee, I want you to take some time and think about Lee's situation. How would you help him? Below are a series of questions that Del will use to help Lee. Write out your answers to be sure that you clearly think through each one. Take the time to talk with someone about this

---

[82] Jeremiah 2:13 "For My people have committed two evils: they have forsaken Me, the fountain of living waters, to hew for themselves cisterns, broken cisterns that can hold no water."

and get their opinion about the hope you will offer to Lee.

What was Lee's fear? Describe Lee's uncertain expectation about Michelle. What errors lead to Lee's expectations? Try to enter Lee's life to know why he would think and believe these errors. What truth did he need to fill his mind with? How might you help Lee believe these truths?

Why is Lee feeling guilty? What is his unreachable expectation? What errors lead to Lee's expectation? Why would he choose to believe these errors? What truth does he need to believe to find freedom from guilt? How would you help Lee believe these truths?

What problems do you anticipate Lee will face in the coming months? How would you try to prepare him for these struggles?

9 OBSTACLES

Therefore, since we have so great a cloud of witnesses surrounding us, let us also lay aside every encumbrance, and the sin which so easily entangles us, and let us run with endurance the race that is set before us, fixing our eyes on Jesus, the author and perfecter of faith, who for the joy set before Him endured the cross, despising the shame, and has sat down at the right hand of the throne of God.
Hebrews 12:1-2

I spent about sixteen years in Arizona. I remember the first time I went to the Grand Canyon. My family walked out to the observation area, and I was overwhelmed. I had to sit down because I was so stunned by the awesome beauty before me. As I sat, I imagined what it must have been like for someone traveling across the continent by horse and wagon. If you suddenly came up to the Canyon, you would be deeply discouraged. It would appear to be an insurmountable obstacle blocking your way.

In ministering to hurting people there are many such obstacles. While understanding that an individual's anger is a result of wrong thinking, we must also take into account the reason for the wrong thinking. The wrong thinking is rarely a single instance of forgetting the truth. Instead, it is a habitual pattern intended to protect the individual from pain. It is time to explore some of the obstacles faced when entering into someone's life to help them deal with debilitating emotional distress.

The Helper

Sometimes the first obstacle is the one offering to help. What does it take to truly help another person's faith? One who will truly help needs to be able to enter into another person's situation. There are two types of errors often associated with this discipline. Some people enter the life in order to see what is wrong. Their conviction is that wrong thinking is sin and sin needs to be rooted out and destroyed. That is hard to argue with. However, in the process, these well-meaning helpers fail to compassionately consider the reason for the wrong thought patterns. This helper might say, "I do not care why you are doing it. It is wrong. That is all that matters." In principle, this statement is accurate, but it is not helpful. To change the thinking sometimes it is necessary to address many other related areas of thought.

Consider the patience of Jesus. He knew the hearts and minds of those around Him.[83] As He walked through the crowd, He was aware of the lustful glances of His own disciples, the judgmental and critical disdain in the hearts of many Pharisees; the lack of faith in those who just wanted a handout. Jesus washed His disciples feet, served them the New Covenant meal of communion, expressed His love for them and then, while Judas was running to the priests to betray Him, heard the rest argue about who was the greatest. In all of this, Jesus was patient. He did not harshly rebuke them. Usually, He did not even correct them. He simply suffered long. Keep in mind that Jesus is God, so every one of these sins was directly against Him.

Paul Miller, in his book *Love Walked Among Us* rightly points out that Jesus looked at people. As he discusses the parable of the Good Samaritan, Miller writes, "The Samaritan sees a person. The priest and the Levite see a problem. They are too distracted, preoccupied, or agenda-driven to identify with him.

---

[83] Matthew 9:4 "And Jesus knowing their thoughts said, "Why are you thinking evil in your hearts? Luke 9:47-48 But Jesus, knowing what they were thinking in their heart, took a child and stood him by His side,..."

Maybe they had neither the time nor the energy to be bothered by someone's troubles."[84]

Jesus saw exactly what each person struggled with, and He addressed their needs. The paralytic whom Jesus forgave thought he needed to walk, but rejoiced to know his sin was not held against him. The woman at the well needed to know that God knew and forgave even her. This truth set her free to give life to her community. We must learn to see what people are facing.

A woman struggling with anorexia needs something more than a proper diet plan. There is a reason why she has developed such a self-destructive pattern in her life. A major part of her struggle is her belief that anorexia is actually good for her. Why would she choose to starve herself? Some people cannot even imagine making such a choice. When someone stops and listens to a hurting person, giving them the respect of honestly considering their perspective, that person is able to speak to the issues that drive the self-destructive lifestyle.

The second area in which we err is by refusing to seriously address the sinful thoughts. Sometimes we are so emotionally touched by a person's struggle that we accept any thoughts the hurting person has as being valid. When one hears of a boy who was molested by his father for years, it is easy to accept his anger, hatred, and deep-seated fear of authority. "Of course he thinks that way. And he should!" is the easy response. It seems that the compassionate person will want to defend this broken individual and never exert any authority. In choosing such a path we are actually imprisoning the victim to a life apart from the joy and freedom Jesus offers. The victim need not remain a prisoner of the perpetrator's abuse. He can rise above it and find the happiness associated with forgiveness. It is essential that we help him make that break. In order to help him, we need to understand the boy's reasons for his sin while still calling sin, sin.

---

[84] Paul E. Miller, *Love Walked Among Us: Learning to Love Like Jesus,* (Colorado Springs, NavPress 2001) 32.

Life Patterns

When entering into a relationship to help a hurting person, it is important to keep in mind that the person you wish to help has spent years developing the thought patterns that have led him to his current problem. From childhood on, every relationship teaches a person how to relate to other people. The dysfunction of his home provides a framework for processing other relationships.

It is a well-documented fact that an abused child is much more likely to abuse his children. A boy who watches his father yell at his mother will likely yell at his wife. This seems counter-intuitive. One would expect a child who has suffered, to be the most sensitive to others. What the intuition fails to take into account is that abuse takes place in a context that the child defines as love.

Years ago, I witnessed a woman striking her ten year old daughter in the face. The mom was yelling at her and the girl was trying to cover herself with her arms. I intervened. The dad looked at me and threatened to attack me. The mom just got into the car. I looked in the back seat of the car and the little girl just stared at me with hatred. I was stunned. Why would she hate me? This event caused me to think for a long time about the dynamics of abuse. The little girl, though abused, loved her mom. She trusted her mother implicitly and therefore interpreted her mother's actions in a context of love. She did not see her mother's actions as inappropriate. It was normal. The victim often feels that they are to blame.

When traveling to a third-world country one faces poverty such as you never experience in America. Your heart is touched, and you want to relieve the suffering before you. In such a situation it must be remembered that what might be poverty in the United States may actually be affluence in another country. What one interprets as suffering may just be normal life elsewhere. That is why children in third-world countries still smile and laugh. They have nothing to compare their situation with so it is just life for them. Without another option, they are comfortable maintaining the status quo. Of course in desperate situations of starvation, this changes. But for many in the world, they are comfortable with their lot in life.

This holds true in the home as well. One's lifestyle and relational patterns are largely formed by the experience in their homes as children. If their parents were critical, they will likely build their lives behind protective strategies to shield them from criticism. If they faced outbursts of rage, their goal will be safety from rage while still resorting to rage to gain their objectives. The life patterns learned in childhood deeply affect one's relational choices.

We need to take this dynamic very seriously. The changes that someone is seeking require a complete transformation of an individual's thought patterns. Just as it is uncomfortable to get a new prescription for one's glasses, this change of thinking makes everything look wrong. We can expect those we help to stumble and fall as they try to implement the new way of thinking. Unlike the prescription of glasses, new thought patterns require extensive effort to follow. We can help as we anticipate the struggles, bring encouragement in the face of failure, and find effective ways to remind the individual of the truth he is trying to bring into his mind.

Unintended Bad Theology: Un-grace

Grace is absent from most relationships. People like those who like them. They get mad at people who disappoint them. Children are told that God is happy when they obey and angry when they sin. "There is no free lunch" and "Everyone is out to get something," represent the cynicism of the day. And yet everyone seems to believe that the highest love is unconditional. Most people assert that they love unconditionally. Unconditional love, which true love always is, is so rare that one can barely even imagine what it looks like. It is almost never seen in this world. It is theoretically espoused in Church, but its existence is blurred by the deep-seated formalism that surrounds it. And yet the Word of God declares, "But God demonstrates His love in this, that while we were yet sinners Christ died for us."[85]

---

[85] Romans 5:8

Worship contains many taboos. Some musical instruments are questioned as valid. Raising hands brings the suspicion of compromise with emotionalism. Dancing is simply excluded, despite the repeated commands in the Psalms. And in celebrating the Lord's Supper, many Christians become superstitious. One cannot smile or laugh. The communicants must be very serious and examine their lives closely in case they have somehow sinned in the last week. Ironically, that is exactly why believers need communion. It reminds them that they do sin, but God unconditionally accepts them because Jesus paid for that sin fully. Another irony is that Christians examine themselves to be certain they are rightly judging the body, but they are unwilling to allow the elements to pass them by because the elders might think they are in some grievous sin.

Grace is an idea that seems very foreign to many people today. Phillip Yancey calls grace "the last best word" in his book, *What's So Amazing about Grace.* In this book, Yancey shows how the word grace touches so much of life, and yet the concept is all but lost. When grace has to be the central idea for relating to others, people feel lost. They do not know how to trust the grace of God enough to rest in Him, and trusting that other people love them even when it is undeserved, seems impossible. It seems absurd to love people who have hurt us. The unintended bad theology of un-grace has destructive results in many lives.

It is imperative that we re-appropriate grace. We need to know that our acceptance by God is based on His grace—not our obedience, or faith (Ephesians 2:8).[86] This enables us to show this same grace to others. Showing grace is an act of faith, trusting that God is at work in the other person's life, maybe working in areas different than we want Him to work. Grace is the power that allows individuals to remove expectations from others. When one believes that she is loved and admired by God, she does not feel the need for others to meet her needs. God is at work in other's lives so we do not need to coerce them to do anything. Grace sets us free to love.

---

[86] Ephesians 2:8 "For by grace you have been saved through faith; and that not of yourselves, it is the gift of God..."

Christ as Mediator

But the bad theology goes beyond un-grace. Another arena of bad theology is how often Christians forget Jesus' role as mediator. Dietrich Bonhoeffer wrote in *The Cost of Discipleship*:

> By calling us he has cut us off from all immediacy with the things of this world. He wants to be the centre, through him alone all things shall come to pass. He stands between us and God, and for that very reason he stands between us and all other men and things. *He is the mediator*, not only between God and man but between man and man, between man and reality.[87]

It helps me to think of another mediator in life: skin. Skin comes between us and everything. Food, a favorite chair, a wife's touch, even the allergens that make life so stuffy, all intersect one's life through the skin. That is the idea of mediator that Bonhoeffer envisions. Jesus mediates between the Christian and God, the Christian and the world, the Christian and the Church, the Christian and the air. He is the only one with whom the Christian may have direct contact. Everything else should rightly pass through Christ before it intersects with one's life. Consider the following example.

For most Christians the happy marriage looks like this…

a Christian man and a Christian woman united in Christ. Analyze this formula in light of Bonhoeffer's comments about Jesus as our mediator. What this illustrates is in actuality an idolatrous relationship. The husband and wife are free to relate to one another immediately, without Jesus coming between them. This is

---

[87] Dietrich Bonhoeffer, *The Cost of Discipleship*, (New York: Touchstone, 1995) 95.

a marriage in which Jesus is secondary to the marriage partner. While at first sight this model looks healthy, a closer look reveals a marriage that will be filled with manipulation. The husband will need his wife to respect him while she will need her husband to love her. Such needs will inevitably lead each spouse to do whatever is necessary to get what they need from the other. Neither is resting in the truth that Jesus, their mediator, provides them with all that they need.

In this illustration, the couple has Jesus standing between them. He mediates in their relationship. The husband is not able to receive respect directly from his wife. It must first pass through Jesus, so that he rests in Jesus' respect for him, not in his wife's respect. In the same way, the wife is never loved directly by her husband. Neither offers love and respect directly to their spouse. It is always a gift given to Jesus.

Consider Ephesians 5:22 in light of this concept. "Wives, be subject to your own husbands, as to the Lord." Focus on the word "as". It is usually interpreted to mean, "in the same way." However, Paul is actually saying, "Wives be subject to your husbands as an act of submission to Jesus." This understanding seems to fit the rest of the context in which Paul lays out God's structure in the Church and in the home. The structure is given by God and the wife submits to Jesus by submitting to the structure He has established. Her subjection then is not a loss of dignity but a noble action to honor her God. She is also not under the husband but only under Christ. Jesus modeled this pattern by offering to His Father the gift of subjection to the authorities in His earthly life.[88]

---

[88] Luke 2:51 "And He went down with them and came to Nazareth, and He continued in subjection to them; and His mother treasured all these things in her heart."

Summary

There are so many obstacles to truly helping people. It is easy to forget what matters and focus one's attention on the temporal rather than the eternal. The life patterns established in the home often serve to form walls that sometimes seem impenetrable. Imprecise thinking and jumping to conclusions leaves many with some unintended bad theology. In addition, the Christian has an angelically-powerful enemy who wishes to enslave every man, woman, and child. This sin-cursed world opposes the truth of God. Finally, believers are broken people with a bent toward sin. Helping other people seems to be almost impossible, but God has given us the ministry of reconciliation. He is committed to making people whole. As you engage in His agenda in the lives of those you love, you will see the victory of God: people created in God's image choosing to trust Him even in the hardest of situations. It is worth it.

10 SELF-PROTECTIVE STRATEGIES

There is a way which seems right to a man,
but its end is the way of death.
Proverbs 14:12

Peter asked his younger brother, Roger, "What are you afraid of?" "There is a horse in the closet." The boy knew the only way to remove his brother's fear was to turn on the light and show him that he was imagining the horse. He had tried to reason with Roger before. Peter told him that horses are nice and he did not need to be afraid of them. Roger was not swayed. Peter asked Roger how the horse could have gotten into the house and where had it come from. Roger was convinced those questions were irrelevant, since the horse was already in the closet. Finally, Peter reasoned with Roger, explaining that the closet was too small for a horse to fit inside. That was exactly what was creepy to Roger. No amount of argument would help. Roger was just afraid, and he needed to see that there was no danger. Peter turned on the light and Roger was able to go back to sleep.

Because of the nature of fear, it frequently overrules sound reasoning. Rational arguments are set aside when faced with something dreaded. Many people are afraid of snakes. For some, simply writing the word "snake" may be disturbing. Other people love snakes. They find them fascinating. They may have been taught to distinguish between "safe" snakes and "dangerous" snakes. Snake lovers are convinced that if someone knows the truth about snakes, they will not be as afraid of them. When it comes to fears, most people are irrational. The emotion is still guided by the mind, but my mind refuses to think truth or to believe it. Thinking truth may lead one to put his life in a dangerous place. Just like Roger, who refuses to admit the fact that a horse cannot possibly fit in the closet because in admitting this fact he exposes himself to the danger of falling asleep with a horse in his closet, people refuse to acknowledge that some snakes are not dangerous, because if they do, they may have to interact with a snake someday. Roger and many others have chosen to place their faith in irrational propositions in order to protect themselves from dangers that they think exist. They choose untruth instead of reality. They hide in a delusional state, paralyzed by the lies they have chosen to believe. They are not alone.

We Want Control

A pastor put a sign up in his home. It said, "There is a God. I am not Him!" As he sought to deal with the pressures of the ministry, he and his wife realized that much of their stress was a direct result of wanting control. People did not act in the way they believed was best. Plans did not work out as they expected. This sign reminded them that God was in control, and He invited them to trust him. By remembering this simple (and obvious) truth, they could choose to accept and face whatever came into their lives.

Faith is hard work. Faith exposes a person to very real risks. While it is in man's nature as God's image to trust, sin has so marred that image that people resist trusting and choose instead to submit to their fallen nature. The choice to not trust is more than an instinctive action; it is based on experiences in life that testify of the dangers of trusting someone. Each person has been hurt deeply. Those hurts warn, "Do not let that happen again!" Like the man who told his doctor, "Doctor, It hurts when I lift my arm." The doctor replies, "Then don't lift your arm." People understand that if it hurts to trust, then one should not trust.

Sources of Pain

Consider three ways people get hurt by trusting: incompetence, unfaithfulness and oppression. Throughout life we face various levels of incompetence. I am not speaking of someone who is completely incapable of doing anything right. I am talking about the "Peter Principle." Formulated by Dr. Laurence J. Peter, The Peter Principle states "In a hierarchy every employee tends to rise to his level of incompetence."[89] In business, a person is usually promoted until he reaches a point at which he can no longer do the job assigned to him. That is his level of incompetence. Every day you deal with people at various stages of this process. You often interact with people who are in over their head. Facing one's own incompetence is a very unsettling experience. It is also damaging for those who have to receive the results of incompetence. Those results range from an incorrect order at the restaurant, to a snippy technical support person on the phone, to an employer whose failures prevent others from succeeding in their job, to a parent who struggles to show her children the love and discipline they need. In all of these situations people learn that one never knows if the one they are trusting is able to accomplish what is needed. The easiest protection is to never depend on anyone else.

This strategy can lead to micromanagement. Some explain to the people around them the exact way to do everything. They assume that others are incapable of doing the job right, so they dictate how it is to be done. This is insulting to competent people. It also demonstrates an arrogance tempered by ignorance. This mind-set fails to learn from others. Since everyone else is incompetent, their way must be the only way to get the job done right.

The fear of incompetence may also lead to complaining. When we expect things to be done poorly, we tend to see things as done poorly. Fear prevents someone from trying new things. "I

---

[89] Laurence J. Peter and Raymond Hull, *The Peter Principle: Why Things Always Go Wrong* (HarperCollins Kindle Edition 2014) 15.

told them to cook my meat well, but it has a little pink in it."
Instead of trying the meat, and discovering that he likes medium-
well better than well, he complains. Such a strategy is again
insulting to others and serves to isolate the individual from other
people.

The second source of pain is unfaithfulness. Every child
faces the sadness of a parent who does not live up to his word. To
the parent, the promise to go to the park was superseded by the
need to cut the grass. To the child, it is as simple as, "You
promised." The little girl chose to trust the promise of her father,
based solely on her confidence in his reliability. When he failed to
fulfill his word, she is left with a little doubt the next time someone
promises. How much more distrust is built when an individual
experiences purposeful deception that causes real harm? The
effect is that everyone learns that they are better off not trusting
people.

The final, and probably the largest, obstacle to faith is
oppression. Microsoft Word's Thesaurus offers three synonyms
for oppression: domination, coercion, and tyranny. Oppression is
the effort to control another person. People, even in the Church,
try to control one another. God says in Galatians 5:1, "It was for
freedom that Christ set us free; therefore keep standing firm and do
not be subject again to a yoke of slavery." And yet, every day
individuals experience the efforts of other people to control them.
Whether the intention is good or bad, oppression opposes the work
of Christ, and it breeds distrust.

The effect of incompetence, unfaithfulness, and oppression
is that men, women and children learn that faith is dangerous.
Each person develops strategies to protect themselves from
incompetence, unfaithfulness, and oppression. Sadly, these
strategies, which are designed to protect one from pain, actually
become obstacles to showing and receiving love.

Sexual molestation of children is far more common than
one would like to think. The effects of such molestation are
devastating because the crime occurs in the context that the victim
defines as love. The guilt of disliking the perpetrator, whom the

child is supposed to love and respect, is intense. The anger can burn for years, becoming a root of bitterness that destroys the victim. And the fear often paralyzes the child as she matures. Each person is unique and develops different strategies for processing their pain and protecting themselves from future exploitation.

Most people have heard that sex crimes are not about sex, but about control. When you take the time to discuss the crime with a victim or a perpetrator you will see how true that statement is. The sexual excitement for the molester comes from their success in controlling their victim. The victim faces an experience in which they are completely powerless. In observing interviews with people who faced the certainty of death only to be rescued at the last moment, it is striking how the emotions flood into their life and they can barely continue to tell their story. At the moment they faced death, they were powerless to take care of themselves. This overwhelming sense of utter helplessness is almost too much to bear. It is also very close to the feeling a victim of molestation feels with every attack. This feeling is intensified if the child reported the crime and did not receive the protection they needed.

How does a person cope with those life-consuming emotions? Two very common and opposite strategies are: to please people or become distant. Some children, facing the emotions tied to molestation, cope by trying to be what others around them want them to be. A people-pleaser becomes skilled at reading people. He will readily affirm people and even appear outgoing even while he is hiding his heart from those around him. That is because the people-pleaser believes that the key to avoiding the helplessness of his past is to be sure people around him care enough to not leave him in such danger. A girl may become sexually active because she is afraid that if she does not do what her boyfriend or girlfriend wants, she will be all alone again without protection. The people-pleaser will often be very open and even share his experiences. This gives the appearance of being well-adjusted. Although the victim appears to have a lot of friends, he has closed off his heart to real love and keeps everyone at a distance, never risking the intimacy that would expose him to the danger again. What he needs is someone who will show the unconditional love of Jesus, a love that does not grow when he does what is expected and does not diminish when he fails. Such love is hard to find.

A second choice is to become distant. This victim decides that she cannot trust anyone but herself. She has trusted authorities and her family before, and they let her down. She will never again be someone else's tool. She is suspicious of people, ever vigilant against another attack. She will experience the well-meaning efforts of manipulation like rolled eyes, expression of disapproval, or even flattery. To most people, these are seen as little things, and they take no real notice. To the victim of molestation, they represent a serious threat to her control. These little relational nuances are seen as attacks that reinforce her resolve to avoid relationship. What she needs is someone who will show her the unconditional love of Jesus. She needs a love that is not offended by her distance nor enhanced by her occasional expressions of love. Such love is hard to find.

Everyone needs to look closely at their strategies. People need to identify their strategies in order to remove them from their lives. The strategy is an idol. It is what the individual trusts to protect them from pain. Instead of trusting God and facing the possibility and the presence of pain, they trust their strategies and run from pain. It is easy to forget that Jesus said, "Blessed are those who mourn, for they will be comforted."[90] Many prefer a pain-free life over a comforted life. But God does not.

As people identify their self-protective strategies, they need to remember that these strategies are actually *self-destructive*. As long as they view them as helpful, they will not set them aside. People must view them for what they are: poison slowly killing their heart by removing their ability to trust. Hebrews 11:6 says, "Without faith it is impossible to please God…" Without faith, one cannot have a relationship with God. Trust is essential to life and anything that undermines faith is destructive to the soul.

---

[90] Matthew 5:4

Our job is to help the individual see and reject her idolatry. The individual will not reject her strategy until she believes that Jesus will protect her. She must believe that He is safe. She must also learn that her fear is not based in reality. This will require her to begin to look at her life through the eyes of Jesus. Seeing that her strategy is actually destructive will help her release it. The final step in healing will require her to believe that God rewards those who seek Him. This reward is not a works-based system. Instead, it involves living within the sphere of goodness where God has designed us to live. This idea will be taken up in the next chapter.

VINCENT L. WOOD

11 HOPE

Now may the God of hope fill you with all joy and peace in believing, that you may abound in hope by the power of the Holy Spirit.
Romans 15:13

Josephine was a young woman who had serious anger problems. Her anger was disrupting her marriage. Her husband, Karl, was not sure if he could put up with it much longer. Her anger, at times, frightened him because he had no idea what she might do. They did not have any children, and he was afraid of what children might have to face with Josephine as their mom.

Pastor Williams spoke with Josephine and Karl frequently. They knew all the right answers. They both loved the Lord. Pastor Williams reminded Karl that he needed to show Josephine the unconditional love of Jesus. It was almost impossible for Josephine to receive this love because she had been sexually molested by her father. She once explained, *"I was raped repeatedly by the one man I was supposed to trust with my life. How can I trust someone else?"* This was followed by a flood of tears.

One night, after an extraordinarily difficult time, Pastor Williams spoke with Josephine and witnessed something amazing. Throughout the years he had called her to reach higher. He never *gave in to the temptation to just help Josephine make life work. Pastor Williams explained that people would fail her, that he would fail her, that Karl would fail her. Jesus had not failed her and she could trust Him completely.*

On this Sunday evening, Josephine understood what the Apostle Paul prayed in Ephesians 1:18-19, that...

> ...the eyes of your heart may be enlightened, so that you may know what is the hope of His calling, what are the riches of the glory of His inheritance in the saints, and what is the surpassing greatness of His power toward us who believe.

On this night, this faithful pastor witnessed the answer to Paul's prayer. The Spirit of God fell upon her. She wept sweet tears of release, trusting that God would never let her go. Today she walks with God and is one of the sweetest, most tender mothers that Pastor Williams knows. It all began on the day that God broke through.

Truth Works

If something is true, it will work. It is not certain that what is referred to as "working" is what one ought to desire. Some parents say, "I tried disciplining my child, but it didn't work." Others say, "I tried praying, but I still felt distant from God." What these people do not take into account is that maybe the action is not designed to produce the result they want.

Prayer is often viewed as a means to great power. By praying, people believe they can get what they want. The family, who hears that a loved one survived a flood, thanks God for answering their earnest prayers. The members of their church rejoice and talk about how merciful God is. God is honored in their hearts. What about the families and churches who prayed for people who did not survive? God uses prayer, but it is not a lucky rabbit's foot to be rubbed when someone wants something good to happen. Christians pray because it is *right to pray*. They pray as an expression of trust in God. Prayer is not a hotline to the Father to tell Him how to run the world. Prayer "works" when it produces in us faith.[91]

Many people build an expectation that some action will produce a desired result. That may work on a computer but not when people are involved. Many parents think that if they discipline their children right, have family worship, go to church, and pray before meals, their children will be good, honest, hardworking Christians. Sometimes the children simply refuse. Is that a failure of the parent, or the method, or of God's Word? The parent likely failed, so it is easy to just blame them, but the rebellion is actually the child's fault. Regardless of the situation, the child is called to obey. If the child fails to obey, he is guilty. To the extent that the parents succeed in implementing Biblical principles in the home, the child has sinned against light, making their crime even more heinous.

Again, the purpose in parenting is not to get obedient children. It is not even to lead the children to salvation. Both of these are subtle expectations that lead people to control their children. The purpose in parenting is to model the love of Christ and call children to faith. The response of the children is between them and God. The parents plead with God to open their children's eyes to the truth and to build in them a passion for Jesus, but that work is God's to do, not the parents'.

The model of helping ourselves and others in this book has been forged through years of carefully studying the Word of God and using it to understand human hearts. The truth works to set people free, not to make life easier. Look at some of the ideas that are central to this model of ministry in order to better understand how it works.

Anthropology: Body/ Soul

The Train model is based on a Biblical perspective of man. Man is both physical/corporeal and spiritual. That is to say that every man is both body and soul. The wording here is important. It is inaccurate to say that every man *has* a body and a soul. This

---

[91] Richard Foster addresses this idea in the Preface to *Prayer: Finding the Heart's True Home*, (New York, Harper Collins, 1992)

latter wording has two errors. First, to say man has a body and a soul indicates that his essence is distinct from his body or his soul. This assumes that somehow, man's truest being is separate from the physical or the spiritual. The second error assumes that body and soul are separate components of man which can function apart from one another. Instead, we see in the Bible that man is both body and soul joined together without mixture but naturally inseparable.

Look closely at the King James translation of Genesis 2:7; "And the Lord God formed man of the dust of the ground, and breathed into his nostrils the breath of life; and man became a living soul." The word "soul" is a better translation than many modern translations which render it "being" or "creature." The word reflects the spiritual nature of man. At creation, man was a physical being. He was simply dust until God gave him a spiritual existence through His own breath. Man became a "living being" when the spirit was united to the body.

Louis Berkhof writes about this unity of the physical and Spiritual;

> On the one hand the Bible teaches us to view the nature of man as a unity, and not as a duality, consisting of two different elements, each of which move along parallel lines but do not really unite to form a single organism. The idea of a mere parallelism between the two elements of human nature, found in Greek philosophy and also in the works of later philosophers, is entirely foreign to Scripture...Every act of man is seen as an act of the whole man. It is not the soul but man that sins; it is not the body but man that dies; and it is not merely the soul but man, body and soul, which is redeemed in Christ.[92]

This theological formulation is consistent with earlier theologians. Wilhelmus a Brakel describes the nature of man.

---

[92] Louis Berkhof, *Systematic Theology* (Grand Rapids, Wm. B. Eerdmans Publishing Co., 1986) 192

God neither creates the soul outside the body nor does He first cause it to exist independently. As the soul is created within the body, it is united to the body with an incomprehensible but essential union so that together they form a supposition, that is, a person or human being...Be careful not to view this union as a matter of indifference, it being immaterial whether or not it is united to a body, or as if it would be better or preferable if it existed independently...In separation from the body, the soul is referred to as an incomplete personal entity.[93]

Whenever an effort is made to separate the physical from the spiritual, injustice is done to the nature of man and must, of necessity, fail in the diagnosis of man's struggles and in the attempts to bring true and lasting change. To remove the physical nature of man or to degrade it by treating it as less important is to deny the obvious reality of one's life. The fact is that people live in flesh and blood. Everyone experiences a real world with real senses. They act in significant ways that they know matter. In this life, people love, which is the greatest thing one can ever do. This love is expressed and experienced in physical bodies.

Greek philosophers, like Plato, found it necessary to separate the elements of man's nature. They equated good with the soul, so that Plato would say, "...the soul resembles the divine; but the body, the mortal."[94] The physical is always inferior to the spiritual. This led to the Gnostic concept of emanations that proceed from god. These emanations span the vast gulf which must exist between the spiritual and physical with God being the purest of the spiritual and man the physical.

To remove or diminish the spiritual is to treat man as an intelligent animal. Whereas man does share many characteristics with the animal kingdom, there can be no doubt that man is superior in every way. Human beings are the lords of creation,

---

[93] Wilhelmus a Brakel, *The Christian's Reasonable Service*, (Ligonier, Soli Deo Publications, 1992) 321, 322

[94] Plato (2009-10-04). *Apology, Crito, and Phaedo of Socrates.* (Public Domain Books. Kindle Edition 2009) 66

able to act as guardians and guides, bringing the potential in creation to its greatest expression (Genesis 1:28). Mankind has a significance which transcends the momentary existence of animals. What people do really matters in a global (and even cosmic) sense.

Recognizing the nature of man as a physical and spiritual being better equips you to address the issues of your life. The struggles that we face are both physical and spiritual. Our spiritual struggles affect us physically, and our physical struggles will often have spiritual indications. These two elements of man's nature also find expression in the concept of the heart as it is found in the Bible. This is the second part of a Biblical understanding of the nature of man.

The Heart

Proverbs 4:23 says, "Watch over your heart with all diligence, for from it flow the springs of life." Watch over your heart. It is important to remember the three areas of the heart as presented in chapter three. The heart is the mind, will, and emotions. The mind processes information. The will chooses desires and expectations. The will is where the heart exercises faith by choosing to act on the information the mind has concluded is true. The emotions respond to the success in meeting the expectations. This is not a description of how the heart *should* work, but how it *always* works. Just as a caboose cannot make a train move, the emotions cannot drive the heart.

The Bible indicates that the mind alone leads. Romans 12:2 says that transformation comes through the "renewing" of the "mind." Philippians 4:6-9 demonstrates the path for change going from thinking truth, to doing truth, which results in feeling peace. We should follow this path because it is right.

Gospel

The simple message of the gospel is that Jesus is all anyone needs. He alone provides the purpose everyone needs in life. That purpose is to honor Him by loving others as oneself. Jesus alone provides the perfect and consistent love people need. Family, friends, church, the Bible and prayer are only tools that Jesus uses to increase our trust in Him. When we see them as tools pointing us to Jesus, we honor Him. When we look to these tools to meet our needs, we will face emotional distress, for God is a jealous God (Exodus 20:4-6).[95]

Essential to the gospel is the idea of grace. God does not meet man's needs because people deserve it. Nor does He meet their needs because they are wretched and needy. God meets man's needs because it is His character to do so. He is "compassionate and gracious, slow to anger, and abounding in lovingkindness."[96] Man's needs are met by Jesus, based on the unchanging reality of who He is. Therefore people do not need to work out some formula by which God will be forced to take care of them. Instead they may simply trust.

The Apostle Paul defines the gospel in 1 Corinthians 15:1-4 when he says,

> Now I make known to you, brethren, the gospel which I preached to you, which also you received, in which also you stand, by which also you are saved, if you hold fast the word which I preached to you, unless you believed in vain. For I delivered to you as of first importance what I also received, that Christ died for our sins according to the Scriptures, and that He was buried, and that He was raised on the third day according to the Scriptures...

The gospel presents the fact that people are broken. They do not get it right. The first proposition of the gospel is the Christ died for our *sins.* No one obeys as he should. In fact, man's heart is "more deceitful than all else and is desperately sick; who can understand it?" (Jeremiah 17:9). When we begin with this presupposition in helping others, we expect to find a tendency toward self-justification. We expect to see a denial of personal culpability. It is not surprising to see that people are capable of

---

[95] "You shall not make for yourself an idol, or any likeness of what is in heaven above or on the earth beneath or in the water under the earth. "You shall not worship them or serve them; for I, the Lord your God, am a jealous God, visiting the iniquity of the fathers on the children, on the third and the fourth generations of those who hate Me, but showing lovingkindness to thousands, to those who love Me and keep My commandments."

[96] Psalm 103:8

great wickedness. That is precisely why people need the gospel. People are broken. And yet they are afraid to admit this simple idea.

In owning one's brokenness, individuals are free to live in truth and free to change. One area in which people struggle is how they respond when they are faced with an accusation. Many times I have heard people complain not about the accusation itself but in how the person expressed it. They are upset when someone tries to hurt them. Despite the rule many learned as little children, "Sticks and stones may break my bones but words will never hurt me," people still ache over a harsh word. They allow another person's opinion to control their emotions.

Consider Proverbs 15:5, "*A fool rejects his father's discipline, but he who regards reproof is prudent.*" A fool rejects correction but a wise man benefits from it. This theme is repeated continually in the book of Proverbs and yet never is the attitude of the one giving reproof a basis for which a wise man listens. The wise man simply changes his life when the reproof is true.

The flowchart below can help process criticisms. It all begins with a simple accusation. Maybe someone says that you lied to them. Too often, that accusation sounds like an attack on your value. If your value is found in your obedience or in the opinions of those around you, it is an attack on your value. However, if your value is found in God's opinion of you and in the unique way that you reflect Him in this world, then the accusation is either information to help you grow or irrelevant. If the accusation is false and you did not lie, then all you need to do is smile and forgive the one who accused you. Their opinion does not match God's and is therefore irrelevant.

If the accusation is true, then you need to ask another question. Is it bad? You may be accused of being fat or skinny. Many people are offended by such observations, and sometimes that is the intention. However, is it bad to be fat or skinny? Not in and of itself. One's weight *may* be a symptom of a deeper problem, but not necessarily. If it is not bad to be fat or skinny, what should wedo with the accusation? Smile and forgive the accuser. If the accusation is lying, surely that is bad.

If it is bad, then you need to determine if you can change. Maybe the accusation surrounds an area of your life that you do not control. If you are unable to change what is true and bad in your life, then you should smile and forgive the accuser. An example of this might be more common for children. If someone calls a child ugly, the child may decide that it is indeed true. Being true, the child can also boldly decide that it is also undesirable, or bad, to be ugly. However, there is nothing that the child can do about it. He cannot change the way that he looks. His response should be to smile and forgive the accuser. However, if the issue is one of dishonesty, which can be changed, then you should. After you change, you should bless the one who took the time to invite you to better honor Jesus with your life, the accuser. Consider for a moment the following illustration of the *Accusation Flowchart.*

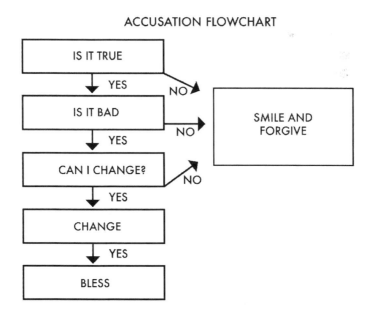

ACCUSATION FLOWCHART

The flowchart shows how to process an accusation. By following the simple steps and answering yes or no questions, one can effectively implement the principles found in Proverbs.

Saying, "I'm Sorry"

Another area in which it is important to own one's failures is in apologies. Often an apology is offered like this; "I am sorry if that hurt you." Or maybe, "I am sorry that I called you an idiot. I did not mean to hurt you." Still another apology is, "I am sorry that I lied to you, but I was afraid you might get mad."

In all of these the one apologizing fails to take full responsibility for his actions. In the first, the one offended is the guilty party for being offended. In the second, the offender is justifying himself. Is it possible to call someone an idiot without meaning to hurt them? What did the offender think would happen?

In the third apology, the offender takes the opportunity to use his apology to confront the offended party for some failure. This is the most insidious of the three because the offended party is also likely an offender. They are probably guilty of frequently getting mad. However, the sin of one person never justifies the sin of another. Everyone is responsible to speak the truth even if another person may get angry.

A proper apology would sound something like this; "I am so sorry that I spoke those hurtful words. I was angry and I sinned against you. I am very sorry. Will you please forgive me?" In this apology the speaker takes responsibility for his sin. He is specific, and he places himself at the other person's mercy. He may face a rebuke, and maybe even anger, but he can face it because he is indeed guilty. Being guilty, he can face the scorn because he knows that, Jesus forgives him fully. If the offended person fails to forgive, it does not threaten the offender. He has all that he needs in Jesus. He can wait for the offended person to grasp the fact that God has forgiven him so the offended can as well.

The Train model provides hope, because it is truth. Because it is truth, it also works. It works, not to make people feel better fast, but to help people face the truth of life and live consistently with that truth. Living in truth is freedom. "It was for freedom that Christ set us free; therefore keep standing firm and do not be subject again to a yoke of slavery" (Galatians 5:1).

12 PROCESS

For I know the plans that I have for you, 'declares the Lord,' plans
for welfare and not for calamity to give you a future and a hope.
'Then you will call upon Me and come and pray to Me, and I will
listen to you. 'And you will seek Me and find Me, when you search
for Me with all your heart.
Jeremiah 29:11-13

The weakness of Christian ministry is that the only tool is truth: truth spoken and truth lived as an example. In helping other people, we deal with ideas. Ideas find their power when they are believed. A lie only destroys someone when it is believed. Truth only sets people free when someone believes it. "For by grace you have been saved, through faith..." (Ephesians 2:8). The work of helping others involves finding ways to communicate truth. It is the responsibility of the one being helped to believe the truth after rationally understanding it and its implications. We cannot make others believe. When we try to make someone believe, or to make someone do the right thing we violate the very freedom we are called to give.

Ayn Rand wrote her critique of religion in her epic book, *Atlas Shrugged.*

> Every dictator is a mystic, and every mystic is a
> potential dictator. A mystic craves obedience from

men, not their agreement. He wants them to surrender their consciousness to his assertions, his edicts, his wishes, his whims— as his consciousness is surrendered to theirs. He wants to deal with men by means of faith and force— he finds no satisfaction in their consent if he must earn it by means of facts and reason. Reason is the enemy he dreads and, simultaneously, considers precarious: reason, to him, is a means of deception, he feels that men possess some power more potent than reason— and only their causeless belief or their forced obedience can give him a sense of security, a proof that he has gained control of the mystic endowment he lacked. His lust is to command, not to convince: conviction requires an act of independence and rests on the absolute of an objective reality. What he seeks is power over reality and over men's means of perceiving it, their mind, the power to interpose his will between existence and consciousness, as if, by agreeing to fake the reality he orders them to fake, men would, in fact, create it.[97]

Rand's opposition to religion, and therefore to Christianity was based on the tendency of religions to seek control: to violate the most basic of all human freedoms, the freedom to think for oneself. Although we may reject her conclusion, that all religion is bad, it is correct that any religion that seeks to control another person; that seeks allegiance without a rational basis, is inherently bad. We offer truth to the mind and encourage people to act upon that truth by faith expressed in their will as a means to heal their emotions.

Repentance

Where does repentance come from? Most children will tell you that if they do certain things, "Mom will get mad." The desire to avoid the displeasure of those in authority frequently directs one's choices. Because of this value, the temptation to focus on God's wrath as a means to promote repentance is a strong pull for

---

[97] Ayn Rand, *Atlas Shrugged* (New York, Signet, 1957) 957

many Christians. In Seminary I preached a sermon in class on Joel 2:12-14:

> "Yet even now," declares the Lord,
> "Return to Me with all your heart,
> And with fasting, weeping, and mourning;
> And rend your heart and not your garments.
> "Now return to the Lord your God,
> For He is gracious and compassionate,
> Slow to anger, abounding in lovingkindness,
> And relenting of evil.
> Who knows whether He will not turn and relent,
> And leave a blessing behind Him,
> Even a grain offering and a libation
> For the Lord your God?

In the message, I focused on fasting, weeping, and mourning due to one's grievous sins. I wanted the class to see how rotten their actions were and that they had brought God's wrath on them.

After what I thought was a great message, the professor stood, looked me in the eye and said, "You are a baby in the faith. When you mature, you will understand the power of God's love and you will emphasize that love." The professor went on to explain that the focus of Joel 2:12-14 is the character of God, "Gracious, compassionate, slow to anger, abounding in lovingkindness, and relenting of evil" It is God's character that invokes great hope in His people. God may relent of the discipline, therefore they can return to Him. I never forgot those words.

Grace

The task of helping people is accomplished in part by showing the grace of God. We, as Christian's, represent Christ to those whom we serve. Our acceptance of the individual must not be based on his compliance with our advice or instruction. Some people will test us. They will purposefully refuse to do the hard work in order to see if we will reject them. They almost hope that we will reject them so that they can continue in their self-protective strategies. When we refuse to reject the one we are helping, we demonstrate our faith in the truths we are teaching. This gives a reason for people to trust our words.

So what is grace? Grace is unmerited favor. Some define grace as "de-merited favor."[98]   At first sight this definition seems like a good improvement, and it probably accurately reflects many people's understanding of grace.   On closer examination, it violates the basic principles of grace. By this definition, creation was not a gracious action of God. Grace was absent from God's work of bringing Adam and Eve to life. Since Adam and Eve did not exist, they could not have done anything to "de-merit" God's favor. The concept of grace as de-merited favor treats grace as a works-based action. It is not shown toward the undeserving but only to those who have "worked" to not deserve it. When grace is based on works—good or bad—it is not grace (Romans 4:16[99] and Ephesians 2:8-9[100]).   It is crucial to remember that grace is *unmerited* favor.

It is the grace of God that we are to hold forth to the needy individuals who come to him. A woman recently mentioned to me that as she tries to implement the principles of grace in this world, it feels like she is walking upside down. Everything around her is oriented away from grace. All of the people in her life are walking according to the gracelessness of the world around them. She is constantly pressured to return to the wrong orientation of life. Therefore we should keep the focus on the undeserved kindness of God. He is not angry when we fail. He does not smile because we obey. We will fail and we need to be ready to apologize, confident of God's mercy. Remember Romans 2:4, that it is not the fear of God's displeasure that changes lives, but "…the kindness of God leads you to repentance."

What this means for you is that his love for, and acceptance

---

[98] Michael Horton, Reformed Christian Resources, accessed 04/22/2015
http://spindleworks.com/library/CR/horton.htm,
[99] Romans 4:16 "For this reason it is by faith, in order that it may be in accordance with grace, so that the promise will be guaranteed to all the descendants, not only to those who are of the Law, but also to those who are of the faith of Abraham, who is the father of us all…"
[100] Ephesians 2:8-9 "For by grace you have been saved through faith; and that not of yourselves, it is the gift of God; 9 not as a result of works, so that no one may boast."

of, the one you help is not based on her problems nor on her success at implementing your advice. The relationship is solely based on the love of God. You should be patient, understanding the struggles the individual faces, as you help her overcome the burdens she bears (Galatians 6:2).[101] We should affirm his love even when others fail. We should consistently remind the person we help that God will never reject her. This will require great effort and a disciplined mind for you. It will also require you to drink deeply of God's love for you. Assurance of your standing before God is what gives you the ability to show God's grace to others.

Black Hole or a Star

Consider for a moment the difference between a black hole and a star. A black hole sucks. Its intense gravity pulls everything near it into itself, even light. On August 12, 2014, CNN reported that "NASA's black-hole hunting telescope has...observed a supermassive black hole's gravity tugging on X-ray light that's being emitted near that black hole." The article continues to explain that black holes "are thought to be formed when massive stars collapse, creating such density that not even light can escape their intense gravitational pull."[102]

Some people live their lives like a black hole. In their desperate search for love and value, they attach themselves to people who best provide what they need. They do not seek to give but only to get. The largest population of black holes are called infants. Infants never seek to provide for those around them. They just want their needs met. This is partly due to the fact that they have nothing to give. They are utterly dependent. Maturity is seen when a child learns to give to those around them. In 1 Corinthians 13, as Paul is describing love and its superiority to the other virtues, he makes this observation in verse 11, "When I was a child, I used to speak like a child, think like a child, reason like a child; when I became a man, I did away with childish things." Maturity is the ability and choice to love; considering other people.

---

[101] Galatians 6:2 "Bear one another's burdens, and thereby fulfill the law of Christ."

[102] Suzanne Presto, "Black hole bends light, space, time—and NASA can see it all unfold" CNN updated August 13, 2014, http://www.cnn.com/2014/08/12/tech/black-hole-nasa-nustar/index.html.

Jesus said in John 13:35, "By this all men will know that you are My disciples, if you have love for one another. Love is the supreme mark of maturity. Maybe this is what Paul had in mind in Ephesians 4:14-16:

> As a result, we are no longer to be children, tossed here and there by waves, and carried about by every wind of doctrine, by the trickery of men, by craftiness in deceitful scheming; but speaking the truth in love, we are to grow up in all aspects into Him, who is the head, even Christ, from whom the whole body, being fitted and held together by that which every joint supplies, according to the proper working of each individual part, causes the growth of the body for the building up of itself in love.

The preeminent example of maturity is Jesus. Jesus says of Himself that, "For even the Son of man did not come to be served but to serve and to give His life a ransom for many." All of His life was lived to give life to others. This is the work of a star. A star gives off light indiscriminately to everything around it. A star does not seek anything outside of itself. A mature person lives like a star. Knowing that he has everything that he needs, namely: the love and respect of God, is able to reflect God's love to those around him, regardless of the other person's response or worthiness.

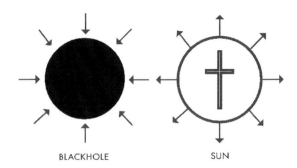

BLACKHOLE   SUN

NO PAIN, NO GAIN

It is a well-known adage that "A person only changes when the pain of remaining the same exceeds the pain of change." Although it is a little cynical, this idea holds some profound truth. For many people life consists of taking the path of least resistance. To experience change, the individual must believe that pain is not necessarily a bad thing.

Why is there pain in this world? Most people think that God's purpose was to create a world, free from pain and suffering, in which man could live. If Eden was God's ultimate goal, the skeptic has a legitimate question, "Why would a good God allow so much pain and suffering in His world?" However, the Scripture does not present Eden as the *goal* of creation. God's purpose was always *redemption*. The angels who remain in their created perfection look with awe at the story of redemption (1 Peter 1:12[103]) . God chose His people in Christ *"before the foundation of the world."* His objective has always been to redeem a people for Himself (2 Samuel 7:23).[104]

So why is there pain? Pain exists to wean mankind from a sin-cursed world. Any loving parent would be heart-broken if his child was content to live in filth. To see your daughter digging in a garbage dump to find the remnants of a chicken leg for her dinner would crush you. To hear her choose such a living condition when she is welcome in your home is even worse. God created man for something more than life in a world ravaged by sin.

This dynamic is seen in Ephesians 2:1-10. This passage is easily divided into three areas. The first three verses describe life outside of Christ.

> [1] And you were dead in your trespasses and sins, [2]
> in which you formerly walked according to the

---

[103] "It was revealed to them that they were not serving themselves, but you, in these things which now have been announced to you through those who preached the Gospel to you by the Holy Spirit sent from heaven—things into which angels long to look."

[104] "And what one nation on the earth is like Your people Israel, whom God went to redeem for Himself as a people and to make a name for Himself, and to do a great thing for You and awesome things for Your land, before Your people whom You have redeemed for Yourself from Egypt, from nations and their gods?"

course of this world, according to the prince of the power of the air, of the spirit that is now working in the sons of disobedience. [3] Among them we too all formerly lived in the lusts of our flesh, indulging the desires of the flesh and of the mind, and were by nature children of wrath, even as the rest.

Verses four through nine describe the work of God's saving grace.

[4] But God, being rich in mercy, because of His great love with which He loved us, [5] even when we were dead in our transgressions, made us alive together with Christ (by grace you have been saved), [6] and raised us up with Him, and seated us with Him in the heavenly places in Christ Jesus, [7] so that in the ages to come He might show the surpassing riches of His grace in kindness toward us in Christ Jesus. [8] For by grace you have been saved through faith; and that not of yourselves, it is the gift of God; [9] not as a result of works, so that no one may boast.

Verse ten points to redeemed man's purpose. "For we are His workmanship, created in Christ Jesus for good works, which God prepared beforehand so that we would walk in them."

There is a Greek word that is used in verse two and verse ten. The word is *periaptéw*. *Peri* is a preposition meaning "around." In English it is used in words like "perimeter" which is the measurement around something. *Patéw* means to walk. *Peripatéw* literally means "walk around in." It connotes living within a sphere of existence. In verse two, that sphere is said to be one of trespasses and sin. Without Christ, people are trapped in a sphere of wickedness, walking about in that sphere accomplishing the appropriate works of that sphere. However, in Christ, people are placed in a new sphere (verse 10). This new sphere is composed of "good works" which God prepared beforehand for believers to walk in. Christians are now capable of walking in good works even while they live in this sin-cursed world.

Pain in this world points people to something better. They

146

long for a place where pain will not touch them. People thirst for a life without death, loss or personal failure (Jeremiah 2:13[105]). God places inside every human a deep discontent with the status quo of sin, in order to invite each person to return to Him (Acts 17:30). If one will quit avoiding the pain by pretending it doesn't hurt, or pretending that it is not that bad, he will run to God with a heart crushed under the unbearable weight of wickedness that surrounds him. He will experience Jesus' promise, "Blessed are those who mourn, for they will be comforted." By teaching people the purpose of pain in this life, we can help them to choose the pain of change over the pain of remaining the same. By willingly facing the pain, they will place themselves in the position to be comforted by Jesus instead of finding hope in their self-protective strategies.

In this way, we help to redeem the pain that individuals suffer. That which oppresses people can be made into a servant who leads them to comfort. People can see pain as a gift from God that will produce in them a character of faith which empowers them to continue on in the momentary existence on this planet. It builds in them the ability to empower other people to find comfort in their pain. It enables people to be instruments of life in a world of death, to be salt and light in a dark and decaying world.

The self-protective strategy is actually self-destructive, for it takes the place of the only real source of comfort. The gospels record an event in the life of Peter that is truly remarkable. Jesus walks up to a boat occupied by the disciples. The boat just happens to be in the middle of the Sea of Galilee. Peter is invited to join Jesus on the waves, and he does. His fear takes over and he sinks, crying out to Jesus to save him. Set aside the miracle of Peter walking on the water. Instead, concentrate on Peter's act of faith and Jesus saving him. When Peter called on the Lord, he was saved. The other eleven disciples did not need to be saved. They had placed their faith firmly in the boat to rescue them from sinking and drowning. Many people will marvel that Peter walked on the water. Some will point out that his lack of faith made him sink. Peter says, "Jesus saved me when I called out to Him!"

---

[105] "For My people have committed two evils: they have forsaken Me, the fountain of living waters, To hew for themselves cisterns, broken cisterns that can hold no water."

This illustrates faith in self-protective strategies. These strategies are the boat which protects someone from the pain of sinking into the sea of destruction. People trust the strategies while watching Jesus walk on the water. They long to join Jesus on the water, but their fears hold them back. They are safe, and yet they never get to experience the miracle of Jesus rescuing them and comforting their hearts. They are too afraid to really trust Him. As people investing in others who are hurting, we invite people out of the boat. We can help them place their trust in the One who will never sink. That is the objective. We must not turn from it to the right or to the left.

Summary
We need to demonstrate the grace of God to others. This demonstration comes through our life and through our words. The objective is to show others that God is truly reliable so that they can place their faith in God. This faith is not that God will make life comfortable but that He will comfort them regardless of what they face.

APPENDIX: DISCIPLESHIP PLAN

For precept must be upon precept, precept upon precept; line upon line, line upon line; here a little, and there a little
Isaiah 28:10 KJV

Have a Plan

"If you aim at nothing, you will hit it every time." The simplicity of this little adage increases its poignancy. Even though most people would agree with the truth it conveys, many still fail to have a plan. Churches have no plan to get out of their self-focused ways and reach out to a dying world. Individuals continue in the same problems they have faced for years, rather than finding a way to change. Some families never seem to move beyond the same old struggles. Goals and a clear plan to reach them are essential for progress. In *Orthodoxy*, G. K. Chesterton gives a picturesque illustration of the importance of an unchanging objective.

> Silly examples are always simpler; let us suppose a man wanted a particular kind of world; say, a blue world. He would have no cause to complain of the slightness or swiftness of his task; he might toil for a long time at the transformation; he could work away (in every sense) until all was blue. He could have heroic adventures; the putting of the last touches to a blue tiger. He could have fairy dreams;

the dawn of a blue moon. But if he worked hard, that high-minded reformer would certainly (from his own point of view) leave the world better and bluer than he found it. If he altered a blade of grass to his favourite colour every day, he would get on slowly. But if he altered his favourite colour every day, he would not get on at all. If, after reading a fresh philosopher, he started to paint everything red or yellow, his work would be thrown away: there would be nothing to show except a few blue tigers walking about, specimens of his early bad manner.[106]

It is important to have a goal when trying to help someone deal with their emotional distress. This relationship has many potential problems. Pride and the gratification that come from rescuing people can cripple the growth of the leader. Dependence on the leader, or gaining personal value and significance only from the leader, may limit the protégé's advancement in his walk with Christ. Both of these sets of problems can be minimized by a clear plan. You will need to know where you are going. Each meeting should have an objective, and the discussion should be guided to accomplish this objective. God may lead in a different direction so you will need to be sensitive to His leading and flexible enough to follow, but such flexibility does not negate the need for a plan.

Consider a six stage plan for meeting with someone in distress. It is unlikely that you can accomplish the goals of this plan in just six meetings. Some people will grasp the concepts after one meeting and will see significant change in their lives. Other people will need time to process the ideas in a single step. You may need to spend three or four meetings at that stage. Keep in mind that this is a guideline and should not be slavishly followed. Know the person you are caring for and adapt the plan to best address their needs.

---

[106] G. K. Chesterton, *Heretics/Orthodoxy* (Nashville, Thomas Nelson, 2000) 261

Initial Meeting

In the first meeting, you will want to lay the basic groundwork for meeting. You will need to explain the foundational truths on which your instruction rests. Two principles are essential to explain at this point. The first is the idea that man is a physical/spiritual being. You will need to explain how the idea of Platonic dualism harms one's life by separating the physical from the spiritual. Explain that people need to do spiritual things naturally and the natural things spiritually. You should emphasize that the physical and the spiritual are inseparably linked.

In the western world people think Platonically. Therefore people often think of their anger as a physical part of their life. They do not see the connection between their anger at being cut off in traffic with their deep spiritual need to be valued by God. Your meetings will be more efficient by setting the proper paradigm in the first visit.

The second element to address in this visit is a quick and cursory presentation of *The Train*. The point is to help the individual understand not only the three elements of the heart-mind, will, and emotions-but also to introduce the way that the heart works. One woman said, "It only took ten years but now I see that *The Train* is not how the heart *should* work but how it *always* works." Be patient, but describe the pathway you will follow on the first visit.

The objective for the first meeting is to present the biblical view of man. You will help your friend understand that the physical and spiritual are interrelated and that the mind directs the will and emotions. Ask your friend to memorize Psalm 73:25-28 before the next meeting. This will introduce the discipline of Scripture memory, and this passage joins the spiritual and physical in a practical way.

Meeting #2

After laying a ground work for discussion, the next meeting can involve an assessment of real and felt needs. As a leader, you will want to begin to develop a hypothesis on the following questions. Where is the individual looking to quench his thirst?

What are some strategies for self-protection, or shields, that the individual has developed? Why did the individual choose these shields? You will not necessarily share your answers at this point. You must also be ready to change your hypothesis as you gain more information. The hypothesis simply gives you an initial direction to pursue.

You will want to introduce the idea of thirst at this meeting. Take some time to demonstrate from Scripture that thirst is not bad. In fact, it is thirst that leads people to God, since He is the One people actually need. You can discuss passages like Isaiah 55, or the woman at the well, in which God appeals to someone's thirst in order to draw them to Himself. For a homework assignment, ask your friend to memorize Jeremiah 2:13. Encourage him to interact with the passage to see what cistern(s) he has built. Invite him to consider how Jesus alone can truly satisfy his thirst.

It is exceptionally helpful for him to write down his thoughts about the passage. Most people assume that they think more deeply about things than they actually do. Writing down one's thoughts forces greater contemplation and articulation of ideas. Therefore, ask your friend to bring a written record of his work on this assignment.

Homework assignments also provide direction for personal worship. Throughout the Bible, believers are warned against the danger of ritualistic worship. Isaiah 29:13[107] records God's grief that His people trust in their activities and not in Him. Jesus reiterates this concern in John 5:39-40[108] as He tells the Jews that they search the Scriptures but miss Him. You can help your friend by giving them assignments that purposefully address real heart issues while they are alone with God. This moves them away from ritualistic devotions and toward a personal relationship with God. Since the problems are primarily related to seeking satisfaction

---

[107] Isaiah 29:13 "Then the Lord said, "Because this people draw near with their words and honor Me with their lip service, But they remove their hearts far from Me, and their reverence for Me consists of tradition learned by rote…"

[108] John 5:39-40 "You search the Scriptures because you think that in them you have eternal life; it is these that testify about Me; and you are unwilling to come to Me so that you may have life."

apart from God, these assignments are even more effective.

Meeting #3

Once your friend has begun to think in terms of his thirst, you can give some more substance to this idea. During this meeting you will want to explain that everyone thirsts for love and value. Discuss Genesis 2:7 and 1:28 in the context of God creating man with needs that are only met in Him. Recognize that women are most keenly aware of their need for love, while men thirst most for value. They still need both love and value but generally their first inclination is in this direction. You can demonstrate this easily from Genesis 3:16-19 where God curses the woman in the realm of relationship and the man in his work.

A helpful homework assignment is to meditate on Matthew 11:28-30. Have the counselee write out each pronoun used in this passage and its importance to the invitation Jesus gives. Next they should write out the verbs and ask themselves what these verbs call them to do. This should encourage your friend to seek the person of Jesus.

Meeting #4

Now it is time to get into *The Train*. The previous meetings have been designed to build trust and to begin the adjustment in the way your friend thinks about life. Now you will talk about how the heart works. As you introduce *The Train*, keep the focus on the fact that the mind *always* directs the will and emotions. He is in control of the emotions that he feels. No one and nothing else can ever make him feel a certain way. Your friend may feel afraid of the responsibility that this places on him. Some people want you to change the situations that they face. Remember, your job is to help them change in the midst of their situations. You need to help them focus on the freedom they have. They do not need to be slaves of the people or situations in their lives any longer.

In addition to *The Train*, you will want to begin to discuss the specific strategies that your friend has developed to meet his needs. Your hypotheses should be reasonably well focused at this point, and you have already helped him begin to see his errant searches for satisfaction. Now it becomes the central focus of your discussions. Show him how he is choosing to trust his strategies instead of God to meet his needs. Give him clear ways that he can follow to shift away from his strategies and turn to God.

An important idea at this point is the concept of "Biblical Grammar." Your friend will habitually place "but" after "God." You will need to correct this habit by challenging him to say "but God." Look at several situations in his life and ask him how it would be different with a "but God" after it. To make this more effective, take the time to discuss the depth of God's rich love and mercy for him. Keep this focus on the personal relationship between God and your friend. He will likely want to talk in first person plural or even third person terms. Help him remain focused on God's love for him, specifically in the first person singular.

For homework, encourage him to meditate on Romans 12:1-2. Point out that God's mercy is our motivation. Have him write out specific ways that God's mercy will help him to seek God personally. Have him look at some situations in his life that would change if he only remembered "but God."

Meeting #5
An important idea, which has been behind everything you have shared with your friend, is the role of the emotions. Emotions are only *responses* to his efforts to meet his needs: to be loved and valued. The negative emotions, anger, fear and guilt, exist because he fails to meet his needs. Failure means that he has not sought to meet them in Jesus, where they are already met. This understanding of emotions should be emphasized in this meeting. You should give the definition of each negative emotion and demonstrate how it functions in his life. Show him that anger is a blocked expectation, fear an uncertain expectation, and guilt an unreachable expectation. Remember each is based on the expectations he has established because of his thinking about his needs.

This is a good time to discuss Philippians 4:6-9. Studying this passage will show that *The Train* is a biblical concept. It will also lay a framework for your friend to process his emotions.

These verses show the progression from an honest appraisal of his emotion (vs. 6-7) to the disciplined change of thinking (vs. 8) to the determined implementation of the truth he now knows (vs. 9).

The homework this week should focus on two passages for meditation, Matthew 10:28 and 1 John 4:18, which both deal with fear. 1 John 4:18 is important to memorize. He should begin an emotional journal. Determine which emotion he faces most often. Encourage him to write out examples during the week when he experiences this emotion. After writing out the emotion and describing the situation, have him describe what his expectation was and why he chose it. When you next meet, discuss these emotions and help him apply the principles of *The Train* to the situation.

Meeting #6

In this last step you can fine-tune the information you have already given. In particular, you can help your friend learn the difference between wants and expectations. A husband may ask, "What is wrong with wanting my wife to love me?" Your answer is, "Nothing. But you expect it because you believe that you need it." The presence of negative emotions proves that he has moved desires into expectations. Helping him grasp this concept is the next step toward freedom. He is able to fully benefit from all that his emotions truly communicate to him.

This lesson dovetails very well with the homework assignment. Go through the emotional journal and guide your friend through *The Train* with some of the emotions listed. What you are hoping to do is help him see his wrong thinking. As he is able to look back over a week and see where he was trying to *get* love and respect rather than *show* them, he is enabled to see this error sooner. Each time a person comes face to face with his sin, he is better equipped to repent sooner. The goal is that eventually he will self-diagnose before he acts inappropriately. Seeing his sin, he will immediately turn to Jesus.

This is a helpful time to introduce the idea of the Black Hole and the Star. When people are seeking to get love and value, they are functioning like a black hole, sucking life from those around them. When they are satisfied with Jesus' love and value for them, they are free to distribute love and respect to others, pointing them to Jesus.

As you conclude this meeting, ask your friend to explain *The Train* to you. Help him to articulate the concepts and the flow of *The Train*. After he is able to share the principles with you, encourage him to share these ideas with his family and friends. This may result in more work for you as people will see how powerful the truth is. They will want to learn more. Now you can start the whole meeting process again, only this time bring your first friend with you and prepare him to care for those in his life by sharing the truth of God's love.

Summary

Ministry is more than simply listening to problems. Each ministry relationship should have a goal. The goal should provide a pathway to walk. We want to lead people to Jesus Christ, who is the "spring of living water" that can satisfy their souls.

Meeting #1—Introduce basic anthropology

Meeting #2—Address thirst and Jesus' ability to satisfy

Meeting #3—Discuss our need for love and value from God alone

Meeting #4—The Train

Meeting #5—Emotions

Meeting #6—Sharing what they have learned with others

Conclusion

National Public Radio's Fresh Air recently did an interview with Charles Blow, a columnist for the New York Times. Blow has published an autobiographical account of his life and the effects of sexual abuse he experienced as a child. This book is entitled, *Fire Shut Up in My Bones*. He described a moment after the first experience of abuse when he considered suicide. He was about to take some aspirin for a headache when he thought,

"Maybe I should take them all and be done with this." Terri Gross asked him, "What stopped you?" Charles went on to describe his thinking as an eight-year-old. He thought of his mother. Would she cry when he was dead? And then a song came into his head. He could hear his mother singing. Blow stopped to explain that his mother would often sing soul music and other genres as well as gospel. At this critical moment when his life was on the line, he heard his mother singing a gospel song. He assumed it must be God and God wanted him to go on with life.

Three things should be noted about this poignant event. First, Satan is real, and he hates us. The idea of suicide suddenly came into his mind. Jesus called Satan a murderer and a liar. At this moment we see both. Secondly, being loved gave Charles Blow the will to live. Our love for one another is powerful. Third, I noticed that this man, who makes no profession of faith, credits a gospel song for saving his life. The gospel is life.

As I conclude this work, I want to remind you that the ideas I am presenting are words of life. As Christians, we are called into the lives of people who are experiencing deep pain. In those moments of agony, we have the power to point them to Jesus—the Way, the Truth, and the Life. When people learn how to believe that God is ALL they need, they are able to understand and trust their emotions. Those emotions will be vital warning signs of forgetting and not believing the most basic truth, the gospel.

VINCENT L. WOOD

Selected Bibliography

Vine's Expository Dictionary of Biblical Words. Nashville, TN: Thomas Nelson Publishers, Biblesoft Inc., 1985.

Adams, Jay. *Competent to Counsel.* Grand Rapids, MI: Zondervan, 1970.

—. *Shepherding God's Flock.* Grand Rapids, MI: Zondervan, 1974.

Allender, Dan and Larry Crabb. *Encouragement The Key to Caring.* Grand Rapids, MI: Zondervan, 1984.

Aquinas, Thomas. "Christian Classics Ethereal Library." *Summa Theologica.* http://www.ccel/aquinas/summa.pdf.

Berkhof, Lewis. *Systematic Theology.* Grand Rapids, MI: Wm. B. Eerdmans, 1939.

—. *The History of Christian Doctrines.* Grand Rapids, MI: Baker Book House, 1937.

Bonhoeffer, Dietrich. *Life Together.* New York, NY: Harper Collins, 1954.

—. *Prison Poems.* Grand Rapids, MI: Zondervan, 1999.

—. *The Cost of Discipleship.* New York, NY: Touchstone, 1995.

Brakel, Wilhelmus a. *The Christian's Reasonable Service.* Ligonier, PA: Soli Deo Publications, 1992.

Bunyan, John. *The Pilgrim's Progress.* New Kensington, PA: Whitaker House, 1973.

Calvin, John. *Calvin's Commentaries.* Grand Rapids, MI: Baker Books, 1981.

Chesterton, G. K. *Heretics/Orthodoxy.* Nashville, TN: Thomas Nelson, 2000.

Clark, Gordon. *Logic.* Jefferson, MD: The Trinity Foundation, 1985.

—. *Three Types of Religious Philosophy.* Jefferson, MD: The Trinity Foundation, 1989.

Crabb, Larry. *Connecting Healing for Ourselves and Our Relationships.* Nashville, TN: W Publing Group, 1997.

—. *Effective Biblical Counseling.* Grand Rapids, MI: Zondervan, 1977.

—. *Shattered Dreams.* Colorado Springs, CO: Waterbrook, 2001.

—. *The Marriage Builder.* Grand Rapids, MI: Zondervan, 1985.

—. *The Pressure's Off.* Colorado Springs, CO: Waterbrook, 2002.

Edwards, Jonathon. *The Works of Jonanthan Edwards 2 volumes.* Carlisle, PA: The Banner of Truth Trust, 1974.

Eggerichs, Emmerson. *Love and Respect.* Brentwood, TN: Integrity , 2004.

Frankl, Viktor. *Man's Search for Ultimate Meaning.* Cambridge, MA: Perseus Publishing, 2000.

Foster, Richard. *Prayer: Finding the Heart's True Home.* New York: Harper Collins, 1992.

Frankl, Viktor. *Recolections: An Autobiography.* Cambridge, MA: Basic Books, 2000.

Friedrich, Gerhard Kittle and Gerhard. *Theological Dictionary of the New Testament.* Grand Rapids, MI: William B. Eerdmans, 1985.

Gaebelein, Frank E. *The Expositor's Bible Commentary Series.* Grand Rapids, MI: Zondervan, 1978.

Henry, Matthew. *Matthew Henry's Comentary Acts to Revelation.* McLean, VA: MacDonald, 1985.

Hulbert, Lee Cox and Marge. *Raised on Fear.* Milltown, MT: EVE Foundation, 2004.

Kant, Immanuel. *The Immanuel Kant Collection: 8 Classic Works.* Waxkeep Publishing, 2013.

Keyes, Dick. *Seeing Through Cynicism.* Downers Grove, IL: Inter Varsity Press, 2006.

Lewis, C. S. *Mere Christianity.* San Francisco, CA: HarperCollins, 2001.

—. *The Problem of Pain.* San Francisco, CA: HarperCollins, 1940.

—. *The Weight of Glory.* San Fancisco, CA: HarperCollins, 1949.

Lundgaard, Kris. *The Enemy Within.* Phillipsburg, NJ: P&R Publishing, 1998.

Machen, J. Gresham. *The Christian View of Man.* Carlisle, PA: The Banner of Truth Trust, 1965.

Manning, Brennan. *The Signature of Jesus.* Sisters, OR: Multnomah Books, 1988.

Manning, Brennan. *The Ragamuffin Gospel.* Colorado Springs, CO: Multnomah Books, 1993.

Miller, Paul. *A Praying Life: Connecting with God in a Distracting World.* Colorado Springs: NavPress, 2009.

—. *Love Walke Among Us.* Colorado Springs, CO: NavPress, 2001.

Moskowitz, Susan Folkman and Judith Tedlie. "Stress, Psitive Emotion, and Coping." *Current Directions in Psychological Science (Online cdp.sagepub.com)*, August 1, 2000.

Nouwen, Henri J. M. *The Wounded Healer.* New York, NY: Doubleday, 1972.

NPR. *Interview with Maya Angelou.* Washington, DC, 1986.

Piper, John. *Desiring God: Meditations of a Christian Hedonist.* Sisters, OR: Multnomah, 1986.

Plato. *Apology, Crito, and Phaedo of Socrates.* Kindle Edition.

Pratt, Richard. *Designed for Dignity.* Phillipsburg, NJ: P&R Publishing, 1993.

Rand, Ayn. *Atlas Shrugged.* New York, NY: Signet, 1957.

—. *The Virtue of Selfishness.* New York, NY: Signet, 1961.

Robertson, A. T. *A. T. Robertson's Word Pictures in the New Testament.* Biblesoft, 1985.

Schaeffer, Francis. *True Spirituality.* Wheaton, IL: Tyndale House, 1971.

Seinfeld, "The Pilot (1)," Episode 62. Directed by Tom Cherones. Performed by Jerry Seinfeld. 1993.

Smith, Morton H. *Systematic Theology.* Greenville, SC: Greenville Seminary Press, 1994.

Smith, Scotty. *Objects of His Affection.* West Monroe, LA: Howard Publishing, 2001.

Sproul, R. C. *The Hunger for Significance.* Phillipsburg, NJ: P&R Publishing, 1983.

—. *The Intimate Marriage.* Wheaton, IL: Tyndale House, 1975.

Taylor, Richard Shelley. *The Disciplined Life.* Kansas City, MO : Beacon Hill Press, 1962.

The New American Standard Bible. La Habra, CA: The Lockman Foundation, 1960.

The Nicene and Post-Nicene Father Volume One. Grand Rapids, MI: William B. Eerdmans Publishing, 1983.

The Westminster Standards. Suwanee, GA: Great Commission Publications, 1978.

Monk, "Mr. Monk Goes to the Circus," Episode 17. Directed by Randal Zisk. Performed by Bitty Schram Tony Shalhoub. 2003.

Walczyk, Chris. *Internet Movie Database.* November 14, 2012.

Walczyk, Chris. 2012. "Top 100 Greatest Actors of All Time

(Thehttp://www.imdb.com/list/ls050274118/ (accessed December 17, 2014).

Watson, Thomas. *A Body of Divinity.* Carlisle, PA: Banner of Truth Trust, 1986.

Wilkinson, Bruce. *Secrets of the Vine.* Sisters, OR: Multnomah, 2001.

—. *The Dream Giver.* Sisters, OR: Multnomah, 2003.

—. *The Prayer of Jabez.* Sisters, OR: Multnomah, 2000.

Williamson, G. I. *The Westminster Confession of Faith for Study Classes.* Phillipsburg, NJ: P&R Publishing, 1964.

Yancey, Philip. *Disappointment With God.* Grand Rapids, MI: Zondervan, 1988.

—. *Rumors of Another World.* Grand Rapids, MI: Zondervan, 2003.

—. *The Jesus I Never Knew.* Grand Rapids, MI: Zondervan, 1995.

—. *What's So Amazing About Grace.* Grand Rapids, MI: Zondervan, 1997.

—. *Where is God When it Hurts.* Grand rapids, MI: Zondervan, 1977.

Young, Wm. Paul. *The Shack.* Newbury Park, CA: Windblown Media, 2007.

ABOUT THE AUTHOR

Dr. Vince Wood has been a pastor in the Presbyterian Church in America since 1994. He has served churches in Arizona, Florida, Wyoming, and Pennsylvania. Vince has a passion for world missions, having led short-term teams to Central America and Africa, served as an interim professor in Africa, and as Team Leader for Scotland. He is currently serving with Mission to the World's Pastoral Associate Couple ministry. All of these experiences helped hone his understanding of Biblical counseling which led to this book.

Made in the USA
Middletown, DE
02 August 2017